PLAYS FROM
AFRICAN TALES

Plays from African Tales

One-act, royalty-free dramatizations for young people, from stories and folktales of Africa

By

BARBARA WINTHER

Publishers   PLAYS, INC.   Boston

Library of Congress Cataloging-in-Publication Data

Winther, Barbara.
    Plays from African tales: one-act, royalty-free dramatizations for young people, from the stories and legends of Africa / by Barbara Winther.
        p.   cm.
    Contents: Anasi, the African spider — Ijapa, the tortoise— Two dilemma tales — African trio — The monkey without a tail — Bata's lessons — Trickster Hare's feast — The great tug of war — Mantis, the dreamer — Two from Abunuwas — Who wears the necklace now?.
    ISBN 0-8238-0296-5
    1. Children's plays, American.   2. Folklore—Africa—Juvenile drama.   3. Tales—Africa—Adaptations.   [1. Folklore—Africa—Drama.   2. Africa—Drama.   3. Plays.]   I. Title.
PS3573.I536P5   1992
812'.54—dc20
                                                                92-3965
                                                                CIP
                                                                AC

To my grandmother,
who told me many tales

CONTENTS

Introduction

Until ten years ago, when it took me all night to fly from London to Nairobi, I had no conception of the size of Africa. Later on, I was amazed to read that Africa has 11,500,000 square miles, is three times the size of the continental United States, and that the United States would fit into the Sahara Desert!

Even more difficult to comprehend is the number of languages spoken in Africa—about 1,000—and at least that number of ethnic groups, each with its own dress and traditions. Furthermore, it encompasses deserts, grasslands, high plateaus, swamps, rivers, lakes, canyons, valleys, snow-covered mountains, rain forests, and woodlands.

I mention these facts because I have heard people speak of Africa as if it were one culture, one sort of place. Those who visit this continent only by way of a camera safari often consider it a land where wild animals are the dominant, even the only interest. Animals are a wonderful part of Africa, but it is the people, the great variety of cultures, that are its heart.

For about 25 years I have studied one of Africa's common denominators: folktales. Africans love stories, especially those handed down for many generations. Each ethnic group has its own tales, but common plots and characters link certain groups. Often there are many versions of the same tale; some themes are found worldwide.

Nighttime is storytelling time. Around a fire, under a tree with a lantern glowing, in the corner of a room where a light bulb shines, in a meeting hall, on a side street, in an urban home—wherever a storyteller sits to tell a tale, people gather to listen.

This book includes a sample of these tales, some altered, for the sake of simplicity, to enhance the flavor of the culture or to fit the limitations and requirements of stage presentation. However, the basic plots, the theme and meaning, and the tone of each tale have been carefully preserved.

I present the tales in play form, because by acting out the desires, fears, hates, loves, and all the other emotions the characters display in a particular setting, you may better understand the accumulated wisdom of the people who passed down these stories. My hope is that after performing these plays you will want to learn more about African people; there is so much more to explore.

My thanks for the help I received from my African friends and all those who guided me along the way.

—BARBARA WINTHER

ANANSI, THE AFRICAN SPIDER

ANANSI, THE AFRICAN SPIDER

Anansi (sometimes Kweku Anansi or Kwaku Ananse) is the name given to the spiderman by the Ashanti tribe of Ghana, and he appears as one of the central characters in the folklore of that country. In the native tales of other West African countries, there are different names for him, but in every country where he is known, the spiderman is characteristically the same—sly, clever, and often full of mischief. (Anansi also appears in folktales of the Caribbean Islands.)

Although Anansi is small, this clever creature can usually outwit larger, stronger animals, and he often enlists the aid of his wife and children in his schemes. Sometimes, however, he gets into trouble and outsmarts himself, especially when he is greedy or pompous.

Anansi, the African Spider

Three folktales from West Africa

I. How Anansi Brought the Stories Down

Characters

THREE STORYTELLERS
NYAME, *the Sky-god*
ANANSI, *the Spiderman*
CROCODILE
MONKEY

BEFORE RISE: THREE STORYTELLERS *enter before curtain. Each carries African rattle. They stand at one side of stage.*

1ST STORYTELLER: We are storytellers from an Ashanti village in Africa.
2ND STORYTELLER: We are going to tell you three stories about Anansi, the Spiderman.
3RD STORYTELLER: Anansi is a sly, clever spider. For this is his way of living among larger, stronger animals. (2ND *and* 3RD STORYTELLERS *sit.*)
1ST STORYTELLER: The story I will tell is called, "How Anansi Brought the Stories Down." (*Shakes rattle and curtain opens;* STORYTELLERS *remain onstage.*)

* * *

SETTING: *Forest of equatorial Africa. Kola nut tree and berry bush are near center. Hornets' nest hangs from*

3

bush, and calabash gourd is on ground. Tall stool is up center.

AT RISE: NYAME *is sitting on stool, which represents his home in the sky.* ANANSI *enters as if climbing.*

1ST STORYTELLER: It all happened near the beginning of time, not long after animals were on the earth. Anansi thought it might be fun to tell stories in the evening. But Nyame, the Sky-god, was the owner of all the stories. *(Sits)*

NYAME: Here comes Anansi, climbing into my sky.

ANANSI: Good day to you, Sky-god.

NYAME: *All* my days are good, Anansi.

ANANSI: But of course. It is only we poor earth creatures who have bad days.

NYAME: I'm not going to change that. If that's why you've come, go home.

ANANSI: No, I'm here for another reason. I want to buy your stories.

NYAME *(Thundering)*: What? Buy my stories? (ANANSI *cringes.*) You dare climb into my sky and ask me to sell you my stories? Great kings have tried to buy them. My stories are not for sale.

ANANSI: Don't be angry with me, Sky-god. I'm just a little spider trying to make my way in life. *(Pleading gently)* Isn't there any way I might talk you into giving up your stories?

NYAME *(Growling)*: What a bother you are.

ANANSI: Why? Because I don't give up easily?

NYAME: Oh, all right, Spiderman. If you can show me a crocodile with no teeth, an empty hornets' nest, and a quiet monkey, I'll give you my stories.

ANANSI: Sky-god, those things don't exist.

NYAME: But if you're as clever as some say, then you can

make them exist. Now, go away. I must plan the weather for next week.

ANANSI (*Pantomiming climbing down*): A crocodile with no teeth, an empty hornets' nest, and a quiet monkey. That will take some doing. (*Sits as* CROCODILE *enters crawling*)

CROCODILE: Hungry! Hungry! (*Opens mouth wide*) I'm so hungry I could eat anything. I'm only happy when I'm eating more and more. (*Crosses stage, peering around for food.* ANANSI *watches thoughtfully, looks offstage, then claps some of his legs together.*)

ANANSI: I have an idea! (*Calling*) Say, Crocodile, I know where you can get a meal.

CROCODILE (*Hurrying to* ANANSI): Where, where, where?

ANANSI (*Pointing offstage*): Over there.

CROCODILE: I don't see anything but a big, green rock.

ANANSI: *I* see a plump juicy frog that looks like a rock.

CROCODILE: Yum, yum! A plump juicy frog. I see it now. That frog is trying to trick me into thinking it's a rock.

ANANSI: Why don't you sneak up quietly on that rock—I mean frog—open your mouth wide, and clamp your jaws shut as hard as you can.

CROCODILE: That's just what I'll do. Yum, yum! (*Sneaks offstage.* ANANSI *watches* CROCODILE'S *actions offstage. Sound of loud crunch is heard, followed by scattered pings.* CROCODILE *shouts from offstage.*) Ouch! That's the toughest frog I've ever eaten!

ANANSI: Aha! (*Calling to* NYAME) Did you see that, Sky-god?

NYAME (*With rumbling laugh*): Yes, Anansi. Greed broke the crocodile's teeth. Now, find an empty hornets' nest. (ANANSI *looks around.*)

ANANSI (*Spying nest in bush*): Ah, there's a hornets' nest. (*He crosses to nest. Sound of buzzing hornets is heard.*)

But it's full of hornets. (*Picks up calabash gourd, takes off top and looks inside*) This calabash gourd looks almost like a hornets' nest. That gives me an idea. (*Yelling*) Hornets, hornets, your home is too small. (*Sound of buzzing is repeated*) See this? I've brought you a bigger, more beautiful home. Just take a peek and see how much better off you'll be in here. (*Holds up gourd. Buzzing continues.* ANANSI *pantomimes watching hornets enter gourd, one by one. He suddenly bangs down lid and buzzing sound stops.*) Aha! (*Calling to* NYAME) Did you see that, Sky-god?

NYAME (*Laughing as before*): Yes, Anansi. Dissatisfaction emptied the hornets' nest. Find a quiet monkey and my stories are yours.

ANANSI: This is going to be the hardest job of all. (MONKEY *enters as if swinging from tree to tree.*)

MONKEY: Chitter, chitter, chatter. Look how pretty I am. Chitter, chitter, chatter. (*Stops to preen and pose*) What a perfectly gorgeous monkey I am!

ANANSI (*Aside*): I have an idea. (*Sighs loudly, in sorrow*)

MONKEY: Hello, Anansi. Is something wrong with you?

ANANSI (*Sighing again*): It's not possible. It simply can't be done.

MONKEY: What can't be done?

ANANSI: There's a great reward for the animal who can stuff its mouth with twenty kola nuts and still talk.

MONKEY: Twenty kola nuts? (*Indicates tree*) Like the ones on this tree?

ANANSI: Yes, and no one can do it.

MONKEY: What's the reward?

ANANSI: The animal who succeeds becomes king of the jungle for a week.

MONKEY (*Excitedly*): Oh, oh, oh! I must have that reward!

ANANSI: But you can't do it.

MONKEY: Yes, I can. Just watch me. (*Rushes over to tree and pantomimes stuffing nuts into mouth as* ANANSI *counts quickly from one to twenty*)

ANANSI: Excellent! Excellent! Now talk to me. (MONKEY *waves hands as if trying to speak, then points to cheeks, jumps up and down with distress, and finally exits.* ANANSI *calls to* NYAME) Did you see that, Sky-god?

NYAME (*Laughing as before*): Yes, Anansi. Vanity made the monkey speechless. I see you understand the ways of the world, Spiderman. From this day on, the Sky-god stories will be known as yours. (*Curtain closes behind* STORYTELLERS.)

* * * * *

II. The First Talking Drum

Characters

THREE STORYTELLERS
FOREST KING
ANANSI, *the Spiderman*
ANTELOPE
LEOPARD
CROCODILE
MONKEY

BEFORE RISE: THREE STORYTELLERS *are sitting onstage.* 2ND STORYTELLER *rises.*

2ND STORYTELLER: I will tell you a story called, "The First Talking Drum." (*Shakes rattle. Curtain opens.*)

* * *

SETTING: *Same as Scene 1. Hornets' nest, stool, and calabash gourd are not onstage.*

AT RISE: KING *and* ANANSI *are talking in pantomime.*

2ND STORYTELLER: In the early days there was one Forest King. When he wanted to tell his subjects anything, it took weeks for messengers to reach the farthest villages. This made the King very unhappy.

KING: There must be a quicker way. What would I do if an enemy attacked? I would be defeated before help could come.

ANANSI: What you need, mighty Forest King, is something to make such a loud noise that everyone in the forest will hear it.

KING: But, Spiderman, I know of nothing that can make such a loud noise.

ANANSI: I can't think of anything either. But I'll have a meeting with some of the animals. We might come up with an idea. (KING *nods and exits one way;* ANANSI *bows and exits the other.*)

2ND STORYTELLER: That evening the animals met in a secret place in the forest. (ANANSI *enters, followed by* CROCODILE, ANTELOPE, LEOPARD, *and* MONKEY. MONKEY *immediately sits down and falls asleep.*)

ANANSI: And so, my friends, that's the situation. We must think of the loudest noisemaker there is.

CROCODILE: Nyame, the Sky-god, can make thunder. That's the biggest noise I know.

ANANSI: True, Crocodile. But Nyame wouldn't let anyone borrow his thunder.

ANTELOPE, LEOPARD *and* CROCODILE (*Ad lib*): That's right. Of course. Yes. (*Etc. Voices wake* MONKEY, *who nods, then falls asleep again.*)

LEOPARD: I have some loud cousins. You know—those lions.

ANTELOPE (*Leaping up; in terror*): Oh, those lions make such frightful roars! We antelope can hear them miles away.

ANANSI: I'll admit your cousins are loud, Leopard. But

I've never met a lion who was willing to carry a message for anyone. (*Animals ad lib agreement.*)

CROCODILE: Sh-h-h! Listen. (*Animals freeze. Sound of drum beating in distance is heard.* MONKEY *snores.*) Don't listen to Monkey snoring. Listen to the drum beating.

ANTELOPE: It's coming from the village. They must be dancing.

ANANSI: Hm-m-m. A drum makes a loud sound.

LEOPARD: It can be heard for miles.

CROCODILE: But a drum only beats out a rhythm for dancing.

ANANSI: Well, why couldn't a drum talk? Different beats could mean different things. And if a drummer were really skilled, he could beat out the sound of a voice.

CROCODILE *and* LEOPARD (*To each other*): A talking drum?

ANANSI (*Waving legs excitedly*): Yes! Yes! That's it! A giant drum to carry messages far away.

ANIMALS (*Ad lib, excitedly*): That's good! A talking drum! Great idea! (*Etc. Noise wakes* MONKEY *again.*)

MONKEY: I wish you animals would stop waking me up.

ANANSI: It's time you woke up, Monkey. We are all going to make a talking drum for the Forest King.

CROCODILE: We crocodiles will find the biggest log by the river.

LEOPARD: We leopards will use our sharp teeth to hollow out the log.

ANTELOPE: We antelope will give a fine skin to stretch over the drum and thongs to tie down the sides.

ANANSI: And I will decorate the drum. What will you do, Monkey?

MONKEY (*Yawning and scratching*): I'll pick some berries from this shrub. Then, I'll sit under this tree and eat them and watch the rest of you work. (*Others sigh in disgust and exit.* MONKEY *pantomimes picking berries, eating, and chattering.*)

2ND STORYTELLER: The animals worked very hard making the giant talking drum. All except Monkey. (*Sounds of chomping, chewing, pounding, creaking, and groaning are heard.*) At last the giant talking drum was finished. (ANANSI, CROCODILE, LEOPARD, *and* ANTELOPE *shove and pull drum onstage.* MONKEY *watches.*)

ANANSI: Now that the drum is made, it must be taken to the village and given to the Forest King.

ANTELOPE: That's a long way to travel.

CROCODILE: This is a heavy drum.

LEOPARD: Who will carry the drum?

CROCODILE: Antelope is the fastest. He should carry it.

ANTELOPE: No! Leopard is the strongest. He should carry it.

LEOPARD: No! Crocodile has the best jaws. He should carry it.

CROCODILE: No! I can't go so far from the river.

ANANSI: Wait! I know who should carry the drum to the King. It should be the job of the laziest animal. (*Animals ad lib agreement.*)

MONKEY (*Leaping up and rushing over*): Now, see here! I don't want to do anything. I don't feel like doing anything. I'm just going to sit here and eat and talk and (*Voice trails off as he sees other animals staring at him*) —and rest.

ANANSI: Well, well, Monkey. *We* didn't say you were the laziest. But you just admitted it.

MONKEY (*Sighing*): You win, Spiderman. All right. I'm the one who has to carry the giant talking drum all the way to the King. (*Starts pushing drum off while others laugh and pat* ANANSI *on back*)

2ND STORYTELLER: To this day the talking drum can be heard in the African forest. And when Monkey hears it, he stops his chattering. He sits still and remembers how lazy he was! (*Curtain*)

* * * * *

III. Tall-Tale Man

Characters

THREE STORYTELLERS
TALL-TALE MAN
LEOPARD
ANTELOPE
ANANSI, *the Spiderman*

BEFORE RISE: THREE STORYTELLERS *are sitting onstage.*
3RD STORYTELLER *rises.*

3RD STORYTELLER: Our last story is called, "Tall-Tale Man." (*Shakes rattle. Curtain opens.*)

*   *   *

SETTING: *Same as Scene 2.*
AT RISE: TALL-TALE MAN *is sitting under tree, staring up.*

3RD STORYTELLER: There once was a man who told tales that were so tall they could not possibly be true. Yet he insisted they were the honest truth. (*Sits.* LEOPARD *enters.*)

LEOPARD (*To* TALL-TALE MAN): Good day, sir. Why are you staring up into the tree?

TALL-TALE MAN: I'm waiting for the magic kola nuts to fall.

LEOPARD: Magic kola nuts?

TALL-TALE MAN: Oh, yes. Last week I caught two nuts from this tree. They turned into two cows. I took the two cows to the Frog King and he gave me two canoes. But two old bull elephants stole the canoes while I was asleep. And so I'm trying to catch some more magic nuts.

LEOPARD (*In disbelief*): That's an unbelievable story!

TALL-TALE MAN: You must believe me, Leopard. I swear it's true.

LEOPARD: You should be ashamed of yourself. I won't stay here and listen to any more of your false stories. (*Exits in a huff*)

TALL-TALE MAN (*Laughing*): Ho, ho, ho! I really fooled the Leopard. (*Looks off*) Aha! Here comes Antelope. I'll fool him, too. (*Stares up into tree;* ANTELOPE *comes bounding in*)

ANTELOPE (*To* TALL-TALE MAN): Good day, sir. Is there something important in that tree?

TALL-TALE MAN: I'm waiting for the magic kola nuts to fall.

ANTELOPE: Magic kola nuts?

TALL-TALE MAN: Oh, yes. Last week I caught two nuts from this tree. They turned into two cows. I took the two cows to the Frog King and he gave me two canoes. But two old bull elephants stole the canoes while I was asleep. And so I'm trying to catch some more magic nuts.

ANTELOPE: What a ridiculous story!

TALL-TALE MAN: You must believe me, Antelope. I swear it's true.

ANTELOPE: Sir, it is bad of you to tell such tall tales and call them true. Someone should teach you a lesson. (*Exits in a huff*)

TALL-TALE MAN (*Laughing*): Ho, ho, ho! I really fooled the Antelope. (*Looks off*) Aha! Here comes Anansi, the Spiderman. I'll fool him, too. (*Stares up into tree*)

ANANSI (*Entering*): Good day, sir. What's so important in the tree?

TALL-TALE MAN: I'm waiting for the magic kola nuts to fall.

ANANSI: Magic kola nuts?

TALL-TALE MAN: Oh, yes. Last week I caught two nuts from this tree. They turned into two cows. I took the two cows to the Frog King and he gave me two canoes. But two old bull elephants stole the canoes while I was asleep. And so I'm trying to catch some more magic nuts.

ANANSI: My, my! Next time hide your canoes so the two bull elephants won't find them.

TALL-TALE MAN (*Startled*): You mean you believe me?

ANANSI: Why, of course. And I'll tell you why. Last week I planted a field of okra. It grew so tall it touched the sky. I made seven hundred pots of soup and fed five villages. But two bull elephants came along and squashed the field with two enormous canoes. Then the Frog King stole the canoes and left two magic kola nuts in their place. I planted the magic kola nuts. And that's how *that* tree got here.

TALL-TALE MAN (*Stunned*): That's an impossible story!

ANANSI: You must believe me, sir. I swear it's true.

TALL-TALE MAN: I won't stay here and listen to any more of your silly tall tales. (*Exits in disgust*)

ANANSI (*To audience*): I have a moral to this tale. He who dishes it out should be able to eat it! Goodbye. (*Starts to exit as curtain closes.* STORYTELLERS *rise and start to exit, shaking their rattles, keeping step to beat.*)

STORYTELLERS (*Chanting*):

Anansi, the Spiderman,
Clever and sly.
Though nobody fools him,
Many still try.

(*Last two lines of chant are repeated until* THREE STORYTELLERS *are all offstage.*)

THE END

IJAPA, THE TORTOISE

IJAPA, THE TORTOISE

When the first European explorers landed on the West Coast of what is today called Nigeria, they were amazed to find highly civilized kingdoms, such as Benin and Ife, where beautiful bronze art objects were being made and life centered around sophisticated courts in large cities. Although these great kingdoms later fell into ruin, many of their art forms, folktales, myths, and tribal rituals have survived and continue to the present day.

The descendants of these ancient kingdoms comprise one of the major African tribes today, the Yoruba, numbering about ten million. Although there are modern cities in Nigeria, many Yoruba still live in small villages and try to preserve old tribal ways. They earn their living by farming or raising livestock. And their artwork, especially wood carving, is among the finest in Africa.

Ijapa, the tortoise, a shrewd trickster, is the parallel in Yoruba folklore for Anansi, the spiderman, in the folklore of the Ashanti tribe, and the Hare, who is the clever schemer in the folktales from other parts of Africa. The counterpart in American folklore is Brer Rabbit, Brer Fox, or Brer Terrapin. Except for differences in the settings, physical environment, and the individuality of the storytellers who draw on their unique cultural backgrounds, most of these animal trickster stories are basically the same, whether they have Ijapa, Anansi, the Hare, Brer Rabbit, Brer Fox, or Brer Terrapin as the main character.

Ijapa, the Tortoise

Two tales from Nigeria

I. The Dancing Palm

Characters

Bussa, *a villager*
Mubi, *his wife*
Bellman, *also a villager*
Villagers, *extras*
Ijapa, *the tortoise*
Yanrinbo, *his wife*
Oba, *the chief*
Attendant
Shango Priest

Setting: *A Nigerian village. There is a dark backdrop curtain with cardboard cut-outs of huts, bushes, and trees. A large clump of bushes up left has vine-like rope hidden behind it. Down left is market area. Right is palm tree with a hollow trunk. Center is Oba's throne-stool.*

At Rise: Villagers, *including* Bellman, Bussa, *and* Mubi, *are buying, selling, and trading in market—nuts, utensils, and cloth.* Bussa *and* Mubi *are selling yams.*

All (*Ad lib*): I'll give you five cowrie shells. No, not enough. My cloth is worth two of your bowls. No, one

17

bowl for your cloth. (*Etc.* IJAPA *enters right, crosses to market, and sees yams.* VILLAGERS *grow quiet as* IJAPA *speaks.*)

IJAPA: A fine morning (*Bowing to each*), Bussa and Mubi. Those are good yams you have there.

BUSSA: Of course. My wife and I grow only the largest and best.

MUBI: But not for you, Ijapa. We know you are a poor tortoise, always looking for free food.

IJAPA: True. (*Spreading arms*) I have nothing to trade for food and no money to buy any. Surely, though, there is no harm in admiring your yams and imagining how good they taste.

BUSSA: No harm. (*Holding yam under* IJAPA's *nose*) I will even let you smell this one. (IJAPA *sniffs deeply and then sighs.*)

IJAPA: Delightful! Ah-h-h, if only I were rich enough to buy them all.

MUBI: Move along, Ijapa. The market is no place for you. (IJAPA *shrugs, looks around, then crosses to palm, sits for nap. After a short while, he is snoring.* YANRINBO *enters right, sees* IJAPA, *and places hands on the rim of her turtle shell, disgusted.*)

YANRINBO (*Yelling*): Husband Ijapa! (IJAPA *jumps up guiltily.*) How dare you sleep under a palm tree while our children go hungry! Where is that breakfast you promised to bring home?

IJAPA: Ah-h-h, Yanrinbo, my beautiful, hard-shelled wife. Well, I—ah—I left the breakfast back there. (*Waves vaguely toward market*)

YANRINBO: Humph! Get your leathery feet moving and hurry up with the food. (*Exits right in a huff*)

IJAPA: I'd better find something to eat. If I don't, Yanrinbo will flip onto her back and wave her feet furiously. And my children will pull in their heads and refuse to speak at all. (*To himself*) Come now, clever tortoise, think. (*Taps head and walks around tree. Suddenly he stops, looks at tree, and jumps as he gets idea.*) I have it! I will use some tortoise magic and turn myself into this palm tree. Ho, ho! Wait until the villagers see this. (*Puts head into tree trunk and raises tree onto shoulders, steadying it with arms. In commanding tone*) Dance, palm, dance. (*African music is heard.* IJAPA *dances with swaying movements, first in place, then crossing to market. As he approaches,* VILLAGERS *resume ad-lib dialogue and pantomime as at start of play.* MUBI *is first to see the palm tree.*)

MUBI (*Pointing*): Look! That palm tree is dancing. (VIL-LAGERS *watch a moment, transfixed, until* IJAPA *lunges at them with a series of frightful grunts and growls.*)

BUSSA (*Shouting*): An evil spirit! (VILLAGERS *scream and scatter, exiting in different directions.* IJAPA *quickly removes tree, grabs yams, and carries palm to original position. Music ceases.* IJAPA, *laughing at his cleverness, exits right.* VILLAGERS *peer onto stage, look about fearfully, then re-enter and cross to market area, backing up toward a central point at which they all bump into each other. All shriek and leap away in terror, then turn and laugh nervously as they recognize each other.*)

MUBI: The dancing palm has disappeared.

BUSSA (*Gesturing*): And so have our yams.

MUBI (*On knees, looking for yams*): Where did they go?

VILLAGERS (*Looking for yams; ad lib*): Where? Not here. There? No. Gone. (*Etc.*)

MUBI: The spirit of the dancing palm tree has eaten our yams.

BUSSA (*Rising*): Too bad, Mubi. We will have to dig more yams from our field to sell tomorrow. (*Blackout. Yams are returned to their original place. When lights go up a moment later,* VILLAGERS *ad lib and pantomime as at start of play.* IJAPA *re-enters, crossing to market.* VILLAGERS *grow quiet as* IJAPA *speaks.*)

IJAPA: Another fine morning (*Bowing to each*), Bussa and Mubi. (*Slyly*) I see you still have those good yams for sale.

BUSSA: These are not the same yams, Ijapa.

IJAPA (*Sniffing*): M-m-m! These smell just as wonderful as the others.

MUBI: Move along, Ijapa. The market is no place for you. (IJAPA *shrugs and crosses to palm tree.* VILLAGERS *freeze.* IJAPA *yawns and sits for nap. He snores.* YANRINBO *re-enters and sees* IJAPA *asleep.*)

YANRINBO (*Yelling; disgusted*): Husband Ijapa! (IJAPA *jumps up guiltily.*)

IJAPA: Ah-h-h-h, Yanrinbo, my beautiful wife with sparkling eyes like ripples in the river. I will bring the breakfast in a moment.

YANRIMBO: Humph! (*Exits right in a huff*)

IJAPA (*To himself*): What worked once will surely work twice. (*Puts on tree*) Dance, palm, dance. (*Music starts.* IJAPA *dances as before. As he approaches market,* VILLAGERS *ad lib and pantomime as before.* MUBI *sees palm tree.*)

MUBI (*Pointing*): Look! The dancing palm tree returns. (VILLAGERS *stare in amazement.* IJAPA *leaps and makes frightening noises as before.*)

BUSSA (*Yelling*): Evil spirit! Evil spirit! (VILLAGERS *scream and scatter, exiting as before.* IJAPA *quickly removes tree, grabs yams, and carries tree to original position. Music ceases.* IJAPA, *laughing at his cleverness, exits right.* VILLAGERS, *except* BELLMAN, *re-enter, and back into each other with shrieks, then nervous laughs, as before.*) Again the dancing palm has disappeared.

MUBI (*Gesturing*): And again our yams are gone.

VILLAGERS (*Ad lib*): Yes. Gone. Not here. The palm tree ate them. Yes, yes. The palm tree. (*Etc.* BELLMAN *enters left, carrying two bells, one large and one small. He strikes them alternately several times, ending by striking small bell three times. Then he stands at right of stool.*)

BELLMAN (*Announcing loudly*): The great Oba, ruling chief, will now sit on his royal stool to listen to the problems of the village. (OBA *enters left, regally, and sits on stool. He is accompanied by* ATTENDANT, *who stands left of stool, holds umbrella over* OBA's *head and waves away flies with palm frond.*)

BUSSA: We will tell the Oba about the dancing palm. (VILLAGERS *nod nervously and murmur to each other.*)

VILLAGERS (*Ad lib*): Yes, yes. Tell the Oba. Evil spirit. Eats yams. Dancing palm. (*Etc.*)

OBA: What is wrong? You all look upset.

BUSSA (*Rising*): Great Oba, for the last two mornings a palm tree has danced into the market. An evil spirit inside the tree has made horrible sounds and scared us away. Then the spirit has eaten our yams and disappeared.

OBA (*Rising in surprise*): Bussa, have you been dreaming?

MUBI (*Rising*): No, great Oba, my husband speaks the truth. We have all seen the tree in the market.

OBA: Hm-m-m. Very strange. (*Scratches chin thoughtfully, then calls*) Shango Priest, we need your help. (PRIEST *leaps onstage from right, carrying carved staff and rattle. He chants with dramatic gestures and dances with jumping and shaking movements.*)

PRIEST (*Chanting*):
> Shango, god of thunder.
> God of lightning, Shango.
> Ride into our village.
> Hear me, mighty Shango.

VILLAGERS (*Chanting*):
Mighty Shango, mighty Shango, hear.
PRIEST (*Chanting*):
Shango's magic power
Will catch the darkest shadow,
Will drive the bad away.
Help me, mighty Shango.
VILLAGERS (*Chanting*):
Mighty Shango, mighty Shango, help.
OBA: Shango Priest, for two mornings a palm tree has danced into the market and eaten yams.
PRIEST: Yams? A palm-tree spirit eating yams? That has never happened before. There is something peculiar about that. (*Suddenly jumps high, startling everyone*) Ha! We will capture this spirit, whatever it is. Bring more yams to market tomorrow. We will glue them to the ground with sticky tree sap and cover them with a thick layer of icky-sticky sap. Then we shall capture the spirit! (*Raises arms at audience and jumps, making an explosive "puff" sound. There is an immediate black-out. OBA and ATTENDANT exit. Yams are returned to original place. As lights go up a moment later, VIL-LAGERS, including BELLMAN, ad lib and pantomime in market as before. PRIEST stands near bushes, carefully watching all that happens. IJAPA re-enters and crosses to market. VILLAGERS grow quiet as IJAPA speaks.*)
IJAPA: And still another fine morning, Bussa and Mubi. (*Sniffing*) M-m-m. These yams have a slightly different smell today and their skins shine.
MUBI (*Brushing him away*): Move along, Ijapa. I told you before, the market is no place for you. (IJAPA *shrugs, then crosses to palm tree. He starts to sit under palm tree, changes mind, cocks ear to right, then chuckles and puts on palm tree as before. YANRINBO re-enters and looks for IJAPA. She peers at tree.*)

IJAPA: Dance, palm, dance. (*Music begins.* IJAPA *dances and makes weird noises at* YANRINBO, *who shrieks and exits right.* IJAPA *laughs and crosses to market.* VIL-LAGERS *ad lib and pantomime as he approaches.* MUBI *sees palm.*)

MUBI (*Pointing*): There it is! The dancing palm! (VIL-LAGERS *scream and scatter, exiting as before.* PRIEST *steps behind bushes, kneels, and peers out to see what happens.* IJAPA *quickly takes off tree and grabs yams. He pantomimes getting one hand stuck, then, in trying to get free, getting other hand stuck, then one foot, and then other foot.*)

IJAPA (*Bellowing*): Help! I'm stuck. (PRIEST *leaps out and dances around* IJAPA, *chanting and shaking rattle. During chant,* VILLAGERS *and* OBA *with* ATTENDANT *re-enter, sneaking up curiously to see* IJAPA.)

PRIEST (*Chanting*):
Ijapa grabs once and twice,
But doesn't know when to stop.
Clever tortoise gets too greedy.
That is why he's caught.

IJAPA (*With sigh*): All right, I'm caught. I promise I won't make the palm tree dance or steal yams anymore. Please, set me free. (*All look at* OBA *questioningly.* OBA *folds arms and glowers at* IJAPA *for a moment, then nods.*)

OBA: Ijapa, I hereby banish you from our village as punishment for stealing. (*To others*) Set the tortoise free. (PRIEST *pulls vine (rope) from behind bushes. He slips it around* IJAPA's *shell.* VILLAGERS *line up behind* PRIEST *and pantomime pulling as they grunt in unison, as in a tug of war. There is a loud popping sound.* IJAPA *comes free and all except* IJAPA *fall over back-ward.* YANRINBO *re-enters with hands on hips and sees* IJAPA.)

YANRINBO (*Yelling*): Husband Ijapa!

IJAPA: Yes, yes, Yanrinbo, my blooming flower of the rain forest. I am going to hunt for breakfast in the *river*. (VILLAGERS *laugh and point to* IJAPA *as he crosses left, shaking hands to get rid of stickiness. Curtain closes.*)

*   *   *   *   *

II. The Bush Spirits

Characters

IJAPA, *the tortoise*
YANRINBO, *his wife*
MUBI, *a village woman*
FOUR BUSH SPIRITS

SETTING: *The Nigerian bush. There is a dark backdrop curtain with cardboard cut-outs of bushes and trees. Large clump of bushes is up center.*

AT RISE: FOUR BUSH SPIRITS *are hiding behind center bushes.* IJAPA, *with a machete in his belt, and a pouch of corn kernels slung across shoulder, enters right, followed by* YANRINBO, *who is scolding him.*

YANRINBO: Ijapa, you lazy tortoise. You should plant cornfields of your own instead of stealing corn from other people's fields. What kind of example do you give our children?

IJAPA (*Waving her away*): All right, all right, Yanrinbo, my sweet, charming honeybee. Go back to our dear little children and tell them their father is planting corn in the bush.

YANRINBO: Humph! I'll believe you when I see the cornfield. (*Exits right in a huff.* IJAPA *looks about thoughtfully and stops center.*)

IJAPA: This is a good spot. I will clear this land and plant my cornfield.

MUBI (*Entering left, carrying jar*): Good morning, Ijapa. What are you doing here?

IJAPA: Hello, Mubi. I'm going to clear this land and plant a cornfield.

MUBI (*Horrified*): What? Here in the bush? Ijapa, nobody farms in the bush. It is too dangerous.

IJAPA: Fierce animals do not scare me. When I meet a leopard I merely hide in my shell until he goes away.

MUBI: I wasn't thinking of animals. Our ancestors say, "Travel through the bush quickly, or spirits will quickly make trouble."

IJAPA: Pooh! Bush spirits won't bother me. (MUBI *looks afraid.*)

MUBI (*Whispering*): Sh-h-h! There are frightful tales of what bush spirits do. (*Nervously*) I have stayed here too long myself. I must hurry to fill my jar in the river. (*Runs to edge of stage and pantomimes filling jar as if audience area is river.* IJAPA *waves as if brushing aside her words.*)

IJAPA: If bush spirits come, Mubi, I will be clever enough to put them to work for me. (*Suddenly, with wild yelps,* FOUR BUSH SPIRITS *leap out of bushes, up center, one from each side and two over middle. Their movements are abrupt, with jumps and hops, and they take funny poses when they talk. Seeing them,* MUBI *screams and exits left.* IJAPA *falls to hands and knees and draws himself under his shell.*)

1ST *and* 2ND SPIRITS (*Pointing at* IJAPA): Who is this?

3RD *and* 4TH SPIRITS (*Also pointing*): Who lingers too long on our land?

IJAPA (*Peering out from shell*): I am Ijapa, a poor, hard-working tortoise with a dependent wife and many little hungry children.

SPIRITS: Why are you here?

IJAPA (*Rising; uncertainly*): Er—ah—well, your land needs cleaning and clearing.

1ST *and* 2ND SPIRITS: Cleaning?

3RD *and* 4TH SPIRITS: Clearing?

IJAPA (*With growing courage*): A powerful ancestor told me what to do with your land.

1ST SPIRIT: Powerful ancestor?

2ND SPIRIT: Told you what to do?

3RD SPIRIT: With our land?

4TH SPIRIT: Could be a crocodile pretending. (*Gestures to other* SPIRITS. *They gather in huddle, speaking so* IJAPA *cannot hear.*) This foolish tortoise is either getting bad advice or making up a story.

1ST SPIRIT: Let us play along with him.

2ND SPIRIT: Yes. Play follow the leader. (*They giggle and nod in agreement.*)

1ST SPIRIT (*Chanting; to* IJAPA): Whatever you do, we will do too.

IJAPA (*Puffing with importance*): Excellent! A wise decision. First, let us clear the brush off this land. (IJAPA *pantomimes slashing away brush with machete.* SPIRITS *watch, then mimic* IJAPA's *movements, chanting, and doing all the work as* IJAPA *watches.*)

SPIRITS (*Chanting and pantomiming clearing brush*): Whatever you do, we will do too.

IJAPA: Now, this brush must be gathered into piles. (*Pantomimes piling brush into several piles*)

SPIRITS (*Chanting*): Whatever you do, we will do too. (*Mimic him*)

IJAPA: And the brush must be burned. (*Pantomimes rubbing flint; in breathy tones*) Tuh, tuh, tuh. (*Throwing up arms; making explosive sound*) Woosh! (*Wiggling fingers*) Crickle, crackle.

SPIRITS (*Chanting*): Whatever you do, we will do too. (*Mimic him*)

IJAPA: Last, the corn must be planted. (*Pantomimes taking kernels of corn from pouch, planting them, and tamping earth with foot*)

SPIRITS (*Chanting*): Whatever you do, we will do too. (*Mimic him*)

IJAPA (*Bowing*): Thank you, bush spirits. (SPIRITS *bow and leap back behind center bushes with yelps.* IJAPA *chuckles at his cleverness.*) Ho, ho! The bush spirits planted my cornfield. Now all I have to do is wait for the corn to grow. (*Claps hands gleefully. Blackout.* IJAPA *exits. As lights come up a moment later,* YANRINBO *re-enters. She stops in amazement, pantomiming seeing a field of corn.*)

YANRINBO: What is this? A field of full-grown corn. How can it be? Ijapa planted it only yesterday. (*Looking at "corn"*) M-m-m, the corn is ready to harvest. I'll pick a few ripe ears for breakfast. (*Pantomimes picking corn.*) Ah, here is a spoiled ear. (*Pantomimes throwing ear of corn into river. Suddenly* SPIRITS *leap out as before, terrifying* YANRINBO, *who drops corn and hides under her shell as* IJAPA *did.*)

SPIRITS (*Chanting over and over*): Whatever you do, we will do too. (*As they chant, they rush around and pantomime picking corn and throwing it into river, then laugh wildly, and leap back behind bushes.* IJAPA *re-enters, then stops, stunned.*)

IJAPA: What is this? My corn stalks grew high overnight.

YANRINBO (*Peering out*): Your corn ripened, too.

IJAPA (*Looking about*): My corn? My corn? Yanrinbo, where is my corn?

YANRINBO (*Nervously*): I picked a few ears, and four horrible bush spirits flew out of those bushes. They picked

all the corn and threw it into the river. (*Points*) They
kept chanting—

IJAPA (*Interrupting angrily*): I know what they chanted.
Yanrimbo, you have just lost my entire supply of corn.
You, you—(*He furiously chases* YANRINBO *around stage.*
SPIRITS *leap out as before.*)

SPIRITS (*Chanting*): Whatever you do, we will do too.
(*They chase* YANRINBO *around in a circle, until she es-
capes, exiting right.* IJAPA *strikes his head with his hands
in gesture of despair, staggering backwards.*)

IJAPA: Oh, no! What have I done? (SPIRITS *see this and
leap toward him.*)

SPIRITS (*Chanting*): Whatever you do, we will do too.
(*Pantomime hitting him on head.* IJAPA *breaks away,
yelling.*)

IJAPA: Help, help! The bush is no place for me. (*Exits
right, running.* SPIRITS *laugh and cross towards audience.*)

SPIRITS (*Chanting*): Whatever you do, we will do too. So
(*Pointing at audience in frightening way*)—when you
travel through the bush, go (*Jump at audience and
shout*)—quickly! (*Blackout. Curtain closes.*)

THE END

TWO DILEMMA TALES

TWO DILEMMA TALES

West Africans are especially interested in legal and ethical problems. Choosing sides on an issue and becoming involved in debating, judging, and solving problems make up an important part of their lives. Dilemma tales are a reflection of this concern.

In these stories, the storyteller presents the basic facts and premises with dramatic flair, using traditional introductions, mime, chants, songs, sound imitations, puns, and humor. The audience participates and responds.

The stories are open-ended, with the listeners invited to solve and comment on the problem. Unlike riddles, also popular in West Africa, the dilemma tales have no one answer. The same basic dilemma tales are told generation after generation, the answers and solutions of the audience changing, depending on the point of view, the times, and the social and political structure of the village. Magic or some special skill is usually an important part of these tales, and some of them are used as teaching devices, especially for young people, helping to establish values and relationships. Other dilemma stories pose ridiculous questions or impossible situations and are told mainly for fun.

Two Dilemma Tales

Stories from West Africa

I. The Snore or the Song

Characters

DRINN ⎫
MUKATA ⎬ *brothers*
⎭
CHIEF
GRANDMOTHER
VILLAGERS, *extras*
TWO SPIRITS

SETTING: *A village in West Africa. Backdrop shows a rain forest with huts under the trees. At left is a small hut with a circular, pointed roof made of palms. Hut has a working doorway and is set at an angle, so that rest of hut appears to be offstage. At center is a stool with a tall African drum beside it.*

AT RISE: GRANDMOTHER *sits on stool facing right.* VILLAGERS *sit on ground, right, grouped about her.*

GRANDMOTHER: Would you like to hear dilemma tales?

VILLAGERS (*Ad lib; excitedly*): Yes, yes. Dilemma tales. I like those. So do I. They're fun. (*Etc.* GRANDMOTHER *raises arms for silence.*)

GRANDMOTHER: As you know, in a dilemma tale there is never one answer to a problem. There may be two or

31

three or more. It is for you (*Gesturing to* VILLAGERS) to
seek out answers.

VILLAGERS (*Nodding; ad lib*): Yes, we know. That's right.
(*Etc.* GRANDMOTHER *begins to chant, gesturing dramatically. She alternates right arm and left arm movements,
keeping time to the rhythm of the following chant.*)

GRANDMOTHER (*Chanting*):
A story. (*Gestures with right arm, then with left arm*)
A story. (*Gestures as before*)

VILLAGERS (*Chanting*):
Let it go from you. (*Pointing to* GRANDMOTHER)
Let it come to us. (*Pointing to themselves*)

GRANDMOTHER (*Chanting*):
A story. (*Gestures as before*)
A story. (*Gestures*)

VILLAGERS (*Chanting*):
Let it go. (*Stamp twice and point to* GRANDMOTHER
with each stamp)
Let it come. (*They stamp twice, pointing to themselves.*
GRANDMOTHER *makes sweeping arm movement, as if
stopping an orchestra.* VILLAGERS *grow quiet.*)

GRANDMOTHER: The first dilemma tale is about two
brothers, Drinn and Mukata. They had left their village to seek their fortunes. One evening (*Crossing up
right and gesturing off*) they arrive at a village such as
this. (*Gestures left.* MUKATA *and* DRINN *enter right,
wearily, each carrying a bundle of belongings.*)

DRINN: It is getting late, brother Mukata. I am tired.

MUKATA: So am I, Drinn. We will stop in this village for
the night. (*Goes to* GRANDMOTHER) Excuse me, Grandmother. May we speak to your chief?

GRANDMOTHER (*To* 1ST VILLAGER): Tell the Chief we have
two strangers in our village. (1ST VILLAGER *exits left,
running. Other* VILLAGERS *rise and cross to inspect new-
comers, ad libbing as they giggle, point and chatter.*)

VILLAGERS (*Ad lib*): Who are they? Probably from a village to the north. This one is handsome. Sh-h-h! Don't say that. Where are they going? Maybe to work in the mines. (*Etc. Meanwhile* 2ND VILLAGER *pantomimes dipping a gourd into river at edge of stage, and crosses to offer it to* MUKATA.)

2ND VILLAGER: Here, travelers, a drink of water from our river.

MUKATA: Thank you. (*Pantomimes drinking from gourd, then handing it to* DRINN, *who also pantomimes drinking and returning gourd to* 2ND VILLAGER. CHIEF *enters left and crosses center, followed by* 1ST VILLAGER.)

CHIEF: Welcome to our village.

DRINN *and* MUKATA (*Bowing*): May we stay the night?

CHIEF: Of course. (*Gesturing to hut*) There is our guest house. However, I must warn you that there is a special law in our village.

DRINN: What is this law?

CHIEF: Our ancestor spirits (*Broad gesture, looking up*) desire silence at night. Therefore, anyone who snores will be immediately killed.

DRINN *and* MUKATA (*Gulping*): Immediately killed?

OTHERS (*Nodding*): Immediately!

MUKATA (*Clearing throat nervously*): Yes, ah—by all means we will obey your law.

CHIEF: Good. Then make yourselves at home.

DRINN *and* MUKATA (*Bowing*): Thank you, Chief. (CHIEF *exits left.* VILLAGERS, *murmuring to each other, exit right, followed by* GRANDMOTHER, *carrying stool.*)

MUKATA: Drinn, my brother, I seem to remember that you snore quite often.

DRINN: Me? Of course not.

MUKATA: Let us *hope* not—at least not tonight. (*They enter hut. Lights dim to show passage of time. From offstage, sounds of jungle animals are heard, then fade out.*

Offstage DRINN *begins to snore.* GRANDMOTHER *re-enters, stealthily, followed by* 1ST VILLAGER. *They cross to hut, listen, then grunt and move away.* MUKATA *peers out of hut, unseen by them, and listens.*)

GRANDMOTHER (*In stage whisper*): He is snoring. The village law is broken. Go tell the Chief. (1ST VILLAGER *exits left.*) The villagers must sharpen their spears (*Pantomimes sharpening spearhead, making hissing sound*), for he who snores must die. (*Pantomimes thrusting spear into ground; exits*)

MUKATA (*Looking into hut*): Sh-h-h, brother Drinn. Stop snoring. (*From offstage,* DRINN *makes strange snorts and grunts each time* MUKATA *speaks to him, but continues snoring.*) Brother, be still. Hush, hush! (*To himself*) Oh, dear, he sleeps too soundly. (*Pacing nervously*) I cannot awaken my brother, yet I cannot let the villagers kill him. I must think of a way to save him. (*Paces*) Perhaps if I do something to get everyone's attention, then Drinn's snoring will be forgotten. But what can I do? (*Stops, as he sees drum and idea comes to him*) This drum. I will play this drum and sing. But *what* will I sing? (*Looks at river, downstage, and gets idea*) About the river. I will make up a chant about animals in this river. (CHIEF, *wearing pouch at belt,* GRANDMOTHER *and* VILLAGERS *stealthily re-enter, pantomiming sharpening spears.*)

VILLAGERS *and* CHIEF (*In stage whisper*): Tss-ss, tss-ss, we sharpen our spears. Tss-ss, tss-ss, our spears grow sharp. (*Lights go up as* MUKATA *leaps to drum and begins beating out soft rhythm to astonishment of others, who look at each other in amazement.* MUKATA *softly chants to rhythm, swaying head and shoulders. For a moment, others stand and listen, then begin moving to rhythm, first their heads, then their shoulders. Next they pantomime dropping their spears, making a clattering noise.*

*They wave arms, then bodies, and finally begin doing a
dance, either rehearsed or ad lib.)*

MUKATA (*Chanting*):
> Down in the river
> Lives tiny old fish,
> With a flippy-flop tail
> And millions of scales.
> He lies so low,
> So low he lies,
> Down in the river
> Over there. (*Points downstage to river*)

OTHERS (*Chanting*):
> Down in the river
> Over there. (*They point downstage.* DRINN's *snores
> grow louder.* MUKATA *chants loudly and beats drum
> hard, with others answering loudly.*)

MUKATA (*Chanting*):
> Down in the river
> Lives little old frog,
> With a grinchy-green head
> And fat, bumpy warts.
> He lies so low,
> So low he lies,
> Down in the river
> Over there. (*Points downstage*)

OTHERS (*Chanting*):
> Down in the river
> Over there.

(Point downstage. TWO SPIRITS *dance in, cross stage, and
exit during next verse, thrilling* VILLAGERS. DRINN
snores even louder, and MUKATA *shouts his chant and
beats drum as hard as he can, with others answering in
shouts.)*

MUKATA (*Shouting*):
> Down in the river

Lives old crocodile,
With a barky-big snout
And great sharp teeth.
He lies so low,
So low he lies,
Down in the river
Over there. (*Points downstage.*)

OTHERS (*Shouting*):
Down in the river
Over there. (*They point downstage. Last shout wakens* DRINN, *who peers from hut, rubbing eyes sleepily.*)

DRINN (*Re-entering*): What's happening out here? All this noise woke me up. (MUKATA *wipes forehead, relieved, and sinks to ground.* GRANDMOTHER *exits right.* VILLAGERS *rest on ground, laughing and slapping each other on backs with sighs and groans of happy weariness.* GRANDMOTHER *re-enters with stool.* CHIEF *crosses to* MUKATA, *who scrambles to feet.* CHIEF *claps him on shoulder.*)

CHIEF: Stranger, you have given us fine entertainment. We have enjoyed dancing and singing. Even the spirits of our ancestors (*Broad gesture, looking up*) came to dance with us. To show how grateful we are, here is a purse of money. (*Takes pouch from belt and hands it to* MUKATA, *who is astonished*) Villagers, since our ancestors seem to enjoy dancing and singing at night, we should do more of it. (VILLAGERS *clap hands and nod in agreement.*) And, since silence at night is no longer necessary, anyone who so desires may snore. (*All rise and cheer.* CHIEF *exits left.* VILLAGERS *and* GRANDMOTHER *cross right.* GRANDMOTHER *sits on stool, facing right.* VILLAGERS *sit on ground at her feet.*)

MUKATA (*Looking into purse*): I am rich! Brother Drinn, my fortune is made.

DRINN: You are very lucky, Mukata. What made you decide to sing and beat the drum for the villagers?

MUKATA: I did it to cover the sound of your snoring.

DRINN: Do you mean that if I had not snored, you would not have entertained the village?

MUKATA: True.

DRINN: Then, it appears half your money belongs to me.

MUKATA: What do you mean? You would have died by the villagers' spears if I had stayed silent.

DRINN: But if you had stayed silent, there would have been no purse. It is only because I snored that you received it at all. Therefore, we divide the money.

MUKATA *and* DRINN (*Ad lib*): I get the larger amount. No, you don't. Yes, I do. What are you talking about? Can't you see? See here! (*Etc.* MUKATA *and* DRINN *exit into hut, arguing.*)

GRANDMOTHER: And now, it is for *you* (*Pointing to* VILLAGERS) to decide between the snore and the song. Should the money be divided evenly? Or should it all go to Mukata? What is your answer? (VILLAGERS *call out answers and excitedly argue with each other, waving arms for emphasis, as curtain closes.*)

* * * * *

II. The Honey Hunter

Characters

TONVA, *the honey hunter*
HEAR-IT-ALL, *his wife*
FOLLOW-ANYTHING, *his son*
PUT-IT-TOGETHER, *his daughter*
GRANDMOTHER
VILLAGERS

SETTING: *A village in West Africa as before. Hut is moved to center, and there is no drum.*

AT RISE: GRANDMOTHER *sits up left on stool with* VIL-LAGERS *on ground.*

GRANDMOTHER: This dilemma tale is about Tonva, who lived in a village such as this (*Making wide gesture, then crossing to hut*), in a hut such as this. (*She points to hut.* TONVA *enters from hut and crosses right, holding stomach as if ill. He has a large honey pot hanging from one shoulder.*) He made his living gathering honey in the forest. Now, Tonva had a wife called Hear-It-All. She could hear the slightest noise any place in the forest. She could even hear this tiny spider (*Pointing to wall of hut*) crawling up the wall. (HEAR-IT-ALL *enters from hut, stops suddenly and puts hand to ear in listening pose. Then she turns to hut, sees spider, and nods in understanding.*) Tonva had a son called Follow-Anything, whose keen eyes could track the smallest animal—even this spider. (*She gestures toward hut as* FOLLOW-ANYTHING *enters from hut on hands and knees, with nose to ground, tracking spider along ground and up wall. He pantomimes gleefully grabbing spider, breaking off its head, and throwing the two pieces on ground.*) And Tonva had a daughter called Put-It-Together, who had the power to mend anything that was broken. She could even put together that spider. (GRANDMOTHER *points to hut as* PUT-IT-TOGETHER *enters from hut and sees spider. She pantomimes picking up the pieces, while* FOLLOW-ANYTHING *snorts, disgusted, and turns his back. She takes magic powder from pouch she wears at her waist and chants, wiggling fingers over spider and sprinkling powder on it.*)

PUT-IT-TOGETHER (*Chanting*): Ekululu jaboluka. Ko de ba, ko de ba. Ekululu jaboluka. Ko de ba de ko. (*She pantomimes putting spider on ground.* FOLLOW-ANYTHING *tracks it as before, along ground and up wall, then snarls angrily at his sister, who smiles demurely and bats her eyes.*)

GRANDMOTHER (*Crossing to* TONVA): Good day, Tonva. Are you ill?

TONVA: Yesterday I came down with a terrible stomachache. I think it was something I ate. My wife Hear-It-All is so busy listening to everything, she scarcely notices what she cooks. Oh-h-h, I feel weak and dizzy. (*Starts to exit right*)

GRANDMOTHER (*Calling after him*): Tonva, surely you are not going out to gather honey today. Not in your condition.

TONVA (*Stopping*): Of course I am. I gather honey every week on this day. Just because I feel ill does not mean I will give up my routine.

GRANDMOTHER: It will be difficult for you to climb a tree.

TONVA: I suppose so. (*Groans with pain, then shakes head to clear thoughts*) However, honey is valuable, and I wish to trade it at the marketplace. (*Whispers*) Besides, I must gather honey before the rest of my greedy family gets it. (*Exits*)

GRANDMOTHER (*Sitting on stool, to* VILLAGERS): And so, Tonva went off into the forest to hunt for honey. Several hours later, Hear-It-All suddenly heard strange sounds. (HEAR-IT-ALL *leaps forward, throwing up arms with shriek.* FOLLOW-ANYTHING *and* PUT-IT-TOGETHER *rush to her, one on each side.*)

FOLLOW-ANYTHING: What is it, Mother?

PUT-IT-TOGETHER: What do you hear?

HEAR-IT-ALL (*Listening intently*): Your father.

FOLLOW-ANYTHING *and* PUT-IT-TOGETHER: Father?

HEAR-IT-ALL: Somewhere in the forest, your father has fallen from a tree. I heard him fall. Now I hear him groaning.

FOLLOW-ANYTHING: I will track Father through the forest

and bring him back. (*Exits right, pantomiming tracking footprints*)

GRANDMOTHER: It was not long before Follow-Anything found his father. And just as his mother had said, Tonva lay on the ground groaning and holding his leg. (FOLLOW-ANYTHING *re-enters with* TONVA, *who has his arm around* FOLLOW-ANYTHING'*s shoulder and is groaning and hopping on one foot. He still carries honey pot. They cross to hut doorway where, with grunts of pain,* TONVA *lies down, putting honey pot down beside him.* HEAR-IT-ALL *and* PUT-IT-TOGETHER *kneel upstage of him.*)

FOLLOW-ANYTHING: Father's leg is broken in three places.

PUT-IT-TOGETHER: Do not worry. With my powers I will mend his bones. (*She pantomimes sprinkling powder on leg and chanting as before.*) *Ekululu jaboluka. Ko de ba, ko de ba. Ekululu jaboluka. Ko de ba de ko.* (TONVA *sits up, feels leg, then jumps to feet.*)

TONVA (*Happily*): My leg is healed. Even my stomach feels better. Daughter, I am most grateful to you. Here. (*Handing her honey pot*) You may have all this fine honey for curing me.

FOLLOW-ANYTHING: But Father, I was the one who tracked you into the forest and brought you back to be healed. The honey should be mine. (TONVA *scratches head, then nods.*)

TONVA: You're right. Here. (*Taking honey from* PUT-IT-TOGETHER *and handing it to* FOLLOW-ANYTHING) This honey is yours for following me.

HEAR-IT-ALL: But, husband, I was the one who heard you fall. If I had not, no one would have gone to find you. The honey should be mine. (TONVA *scratches head, then nods.*)

TONVA: You're right. (*Taking honey from* FOLLOW-ANYTHING *and handing it to* HEAR-IT-ALL) You may have it all for hearing me. (*Others protest, waving arms and shaking fists. Family argues loudly.*)

ALL (*Ad lib*): The honey should be mine. Mine. Divide it three ways. No, four. No, two. No, no! (*Etc. Finally, TONVA grabs honey and exits into hut, followed by rest of family, still arguing.*)

GRANDMOTHER (*Pointing to VILLAGERS*): And now, it is time for you to decide. Who should get the honey? The hunter, the listener, the follower, or the healer? Should the honey be divided evenly? What is your answer? (*VILLAGERS excitedly call out answers as before. Meanwhile, curtain starts to close. Just before it closes completely GRANDMOTHER peeks out at audience, pointing at them and shouting*) What do you people think? (*Curtain closes.*)

THE END

AFRICAN TRIO

AFRICAN TRIO

In most parts of Africa, there are still storytellers who go from village to village telling tales, usually at night and around a fire. Animals are popular characters in their tales, especially clever little creatures who fool and outwit larger, stronger ones. Some stories are used to teach a moral; others are told for sheer entertainment.

In the first tale of "African Trio," the tiny Caterpillar fools Hare, Leopard, Rhinoceros, and Elephant. However, little Frog fools Caterpillar, not only because he is more clever, but also because Caterpillar has pushed his luck too far.

The second tale is an African myth about Hare, the hero-trickster of many tribal stories in which there is a struggle against nature for survival. The listeners identify with the small creature, who triumphs over the greater force.

The theme of the third tale is a familar one in world folklore: if you do not have inner beauty, your outward beauty will become ugly. This story also teaches that truth and knowledge should not be hidden.

African Trio

Tales from East, South and West Africa

I. The Fierce Creature

Characters

THREE STORYTELLERS
CATERPILLAR
HARE
LEOPARD
RHINOCEROS
ELEPHANT
FROG
STAGEHAND

BEFORE RISE: THREE STORYTELLERS *enter before curtain and sit on three stools at left.* 2ND STORYTELLER *beats African drum during opening lines.*

1ST STORYTELLER: Listen!
3RD STORYTELLER: Listen!
2ND STORYTELLER: Listen to a continent!
1ST STORYTELLER: Listen!
1ST *and* 3RD STORYTELLERS: Listen!
ALL: Listen to the rhythm. Boom, boom, boom, boom. Boomity boom, boom, boom.
2ND STORYTELLER: African beat! (1ST *and* 3RD STORYTELLERS *slap thighs.*) Up through your feet! (*All stamp feet*)
1ST *and* 3RD STORYTELLERS: Telling the folktales . . .

45

2ND STORYTELLER: Native, tribal folktales . . .

ALL: Of—(*They pause, then shout.*) Africa! (2ND STORY-
TELLER *stops beating drum.*)

1ST STORYTELLER (*Rising*): The story I shall tell you is
from East Africa. It is told by the tall Masai who live
in the high country of Kenya. It is the story of "The
Fierce Creature." (*Curtain opens.*)

* * *

SETTING: *The stage is bare. A slide of East Africa is projected on the screen which serves as a backdrop.*

AT RISE: STAGEHAND *carries on a large cut-out of a Masai
house (see Production Notes) and exits.*

1ST STORYTELLER: A caterpillar came crawling along, looking for a place to rest. He entered the house of the hare.
(*As he speaks,* CATERPILLAR *crawls onstage and behind
house.*) When the hare came home, he noticed strange
marks on the ground in front of his house. (HARE *enters
and inspects ground in front of house.*)

HARE (*Shouting*): Who is in my house?

1ST STORYTELLER: The caterpillar did not want to be
eaten by the hare, so he answered in a fierce voice.

CATERPILLAR (*From behind house*): I am the terrible warrior, deadlier than the leopard. I crush the rhinoceros
to earth and trample the mighty elephant.

1ST STORYTELLER: The hare was most frightened. (HARE
hops about and trembles.) He didn't know what to do,
so when the leopard came padding by, searching for
meat, the hare stopped her. (LEOPARD *roars off left, then
enters stealthily, sniffing wind.*)

HARE: There is a fierce creature in my house, leopard.
(LEOPARD *crosses to house, sniffing stage.*)

LEOPARD (*Loudly*): Who is in the hare's house?

CATERPILLAR (*From behind house; fiercely*): I am the terrible warrior, deadlier than the leopard. I crush the

rhinoceros to earth and trample the mighty elephant. (LEOPARD *yelps in fear and hides behind* HARE.)

1ST STORYTELLER: Soon a rhinoceros came charging by on his way to the water hole. (RHINOCEROS *snorts off left and enters, charging, with his horn lowered.*)

HARE: Can you help me, rhinoceros? There is a fierce creature in my house. (RHINOCEROS *snorts, then charges to* HARE's *house.*)

RHINOCEROS (*Loudly*): Who is in the hare's house?

CATERPILLAR (*From behind house; fiercely*): I am the terrible warrior, deadlier than the leopard. I crush the rhinoceros to earth and trample the mighty elephant. (RHINOCEROS *snorts in fear and hides behind* LEOPARD.)

1ST STORYTELLER: Soon an elephant came lumbering by, looking for bananas. (ELEPHANT *trumpets off left, then lumbers in, pantomiming looking in trees for bananas.*)

HARE: Can you help us, elephant? There is a fierce creature in my house. (ELEPHANT *lumbers to house.*)

ELEPHANT (*Loudly*): Who is in the hare's house?

CATERPILLAR (*From behind house; fiercely*): I am the terrible warrior, deadlier than the leopard. I crush the rhinoceros to earth, and trample the mighty elephant. (ELEPHANT *trumpets in fear and hides behind* RHINOCEROS.)

1ST STORYTELLER: Finally, a clever frog came hopping by on his way to catch bugs. (FROG *croaks offstage and enters, hopping.*)

HARE: Frog, can you help me? There is a fierce creature in my house. (FROG *hops to house.*)

FROG: Who is in the hare's house?

CATERPILLAR (*From behind house; fiercely*): I am the terrible warrior, deadlier than the leopard. I crush the rhinoceros to earth and trample the mighty elephant.

FROG (*Shouting*): I, the hideous leaper, have come. I am slimy, green and full of great big warts. (CATERPILLAR *squeaks in fear, crawls out from behind* HARE's *house and off right.*)

CATERPILLAR (*Exiting*): Help! Help! (*Animals watch him go, then fall down, laughing.*)

FROG (*Bowing*): Kindly excuse me. I believe I just saw a fierce creature come crawling out of the hare's house. I, the terrible warrior, will pursue him, for my dinner is long overdue. (*Exits right, hopping;* 1ST STORYTELLER *sits. Curtain*)

*   *   *   *   *

II.   When the Hare Brought the Sun

Characters

THREE STORYTELLERS
HEADMAN
CHIEF
SUN GIRL
MOON GIRL
HARE
PURSUERS, *animals from first play or extras*
STAGEHAND

BEFORE RISE: THREE STORYTELLERS *remain seated.* 2ND STORYTELLER *begins to beat drum.*

1ST STORYTELLER: Listen!
3RD STORYTELLER: Listen!
2ND STORYTELLER: Listen to a continent.
1ST STORYTELLER: Listen!
1ST *and* 3RD STORYTELLERS: Listen!
ALL: Listen to the rhythm. Boom, boom, boom, boom. Boomity boom, boom, boom.
2ND STORYTELLER: African beat! (1ST *and* 3RD STORYTELLERS *slap thighs.*) Up through your feet! (*All stamp feet.*)
1ST *and* 3RD STORYTELLERS: Telling the folktales . . .

2ND STORYTELLER: Native, tribal folktales . . .

ALL: Of—(*Pause, then shout*) Africa! (*Drum stops.*)

2ND STORYTELLER (*Rising*): I shall tell another story of the hare. It is told among the tribes who live on the flat grasslands of the veld in South Africa. It is called, "When the Hare Brought the Sun." (*Curtain opens.*)

* * *

SETTING: *Bare stage. A view of South Africa is projected on the screen.*

AT RISE: 2ND STORYTELLER *begins narration.*

2ND STORYTELLER: In the early days when the earth had no sun or moon, the hare took his musical instrument called the mbira and climbed up a giant spider web to visit the great country which was up above. (HARE *enters, playing mbira, or another simple stringed instrument.*) He came to the village, seeking shelter. (STAGEHAND *carries on cut-out of veld house, with working door, and exits.* NOTE: *See Production Notes for house description.*)

HARE (*Looking at house, then calling loudly*): Where is the chief?

HEADMAN (*Entering right*): I am the headman of this village. Why do you wish to see the chief?

HARE: I will play my instrument for him if he gives me shelter.

HEADMAN (*Calling off right*): Great chief, there is a hare who comes to our village playing the mbira. He seeks shelter.

CHIEF (*Entering right; to* HARE): Play for me. (HARE *plays instrument and dances.*) You play well. I shall give you lodging in this house. (*Points to house*)

HARE: Thank you. I have had a tiring journey. It will be good to rest. (CHIEF *and* HEADMAN *exit.* HARE *enters house.*)

2ND STORYTELLER: That evening the hare looked out of his door and saw a girl sitting in front of two large pots. (MOON GIRL *enters right with a large red pot and a large yellow pot. She sits and places pots before her.* HARE *peers out of door and watches. Suddenly,* SUN GIRL *enters, running, carrying a large red disc.*)

SUN GIRL: I bring the sun back from our sky. (*Puts disc into red pot*)

MOON GIRL: Then it is time for me to hang out the moon. (*Takes yellow disc from yellow pot and exits*)

SUN GIRL: It is time for me to go to bed. (*Yawns and exits*)

HARE (*Creeping out of house*): It would be a fine thing for my world below to have some of that sun. (*He takes red disc from red pot and tears off a piece of it.*) I'll climb back down the spider web to earth. (*Runs off right*)

2ND STORYTELLER: The next morning the two girls returned.

MOON GIRL (*Entering left with yellow disc*): It is time for me to rest. (*Puts yellow disc in yellow pot*)

SUN GIRL (*Entering*): It is time for me to hang out the sun. (*Reaches into red pot*) Something is wrong with the sun! (*Pulls out torn disc*) Look! Part of it is missing. (*Loudly*) Someone has stolen part of the sun! (HEADMAN *and* CHIEF *rush on from right.*)

CHIEF: How dare anybody do such a thing?

HEADMAN (*Looking at ground and pointing*): It must have been the hare. These are his footprints.

CHIEF: We shall follow him. (CHIEF *and* HEADMAN *exit left, running.* SUN GIRL *and* MOON GIRL *follow, carrying pots.* STAGEHAND *enters and removes house.*)

2ND STORYTELLER: The chief and his headman climbed down the great spider web to earth, and called together the animals to pursue the hare. (HARE *enters left and runs across stage in slow motion.* CHIEF, HEADMAN *and* PURSUERS—*animals from first play—enter left in single file and run after* HARE, *also in slow motion*) As the pursuers drew closer, the hare threw the three-spiked devil thorns across his trail. (HARE *pantomimes throwing thorns.* CHIEF, HEADMAN *and* PURSUERS *cry out in pain as they step on "thorns," rub feet or paws, and continue to track* HARE.) The hare pulled down huge vines to block his path. (HARE *pantomimes pulling down vines, and others pantomime fighting through them.*) The hare caused a great rain to wash away his footprints. (HARE *points to sky and others cover heads with hands, peering closer to ground.*) The hare came to a stream. He lay down and turned into a log. (HARE *lies down and remains motionless.*)

CHIEF (*Stopping and looking around*): I don't see the hare's footprints anymore.

HEADMAN: Neither do I.

1ST PURSUER (*Sniffing*): We don't smell him, either.

CHIEF: I guess we've lost him. Come on, let's go home. (*In single file,* CHIEF, HEADMAN *and* PURSUERS *pretend to walk across "log" and exit.* HARE *jumps up and leaps for joy.*)

2ND STORYTELLER: So the hare gave the sun to the earth, and we have had it ever since that day. (HARE *waves "sun" as curtain closes.*)

* * * * *

III.   The Princess Who Was Hidden from the World

Characters

THREE STORYTELLERS
OLD CHIEF
PRINCESS
YOUNG CHIEF
SERVANT GIRL
EMISSARY
PROPERTY GIRL

BEFORE RISE: 2ND STORYTELLER *beats drum.*

1ST STORYTELLER: Listen!

3RD STORYTELLER: Listen!

2ND STORYTELLER: Listen to a continent.

1ST STORYTELLER: Listen!

1ST *and* 3RD STORYTELLERS: Listen!

ALL: Listen to the rhythm. Boom, boom, boom, boom. Boomity boom, boom, boom.

2ND STORYTELLER: African beat! (1ST *and* 3RD STORYTELLERS *slap thighs.*) Up through your feet! (*All stamp feet.*)

1ST *and* 3RD STORYTELLERS: Telling the folktales . . .

2ND STORYTELLER: Native, tribal folktales . . .

ALL: Of—(*Pause, then shout*) Africa! (*Drum stops.*)

3RD STORYTELLER (*Standing*): The story I shall tell you is from West Africa. It is told by the Vai tribe in the rain forests of Liberia. The name of the story is "The Princess Who Was Hidden from the World." (*Curtains open.*)

* * *

SETTING: *Slide of Liberia is projected on screen. Liberian house is at right (see Production Notes).*

AT RISE: OLD CHIEF *enters.*

3RD STORYTELLER: There was an old chief who was very good but not very wise. He had a beautiful daughter. (PRINCESS *enters and stands by* OLD CHIEF.) Although she was well trained at being a princess (PRINCESS *poses gracefully.*), she was kept hidden away from the world. (OLD CHIEF *puts his hand over his daughter's eyes and peers about suspiciously.*) The young chief of another tribe heard about this lovely girl. (YOUNG CHIEF *and* EMISSARY *enter at left.*) He sent an emissary with gifts and an offer of marriage. (YOUNG CHIEF *pantomimes handing gifts to* EMISSARY, *who staggers under their weight, then crosses to* OLD CHIEF.) The old chief agreed to the marriage. (OLD CHIEF *nods as he examines gifts.* EMISSARY *and* YOUNG CHIEF *exit.*) He called for a servant girl to take his daughter to marry the young tribal chief. (OLD CHIEF *beckons off right.* SERVANT GIRL *enters and takes* PRINCESS'S *hand.* OLD CHIEF *smiles happily and exits.*) The servant girl and the princess traveled through the rain forest. (PRINCESS *follows* SERVANT GIRL *offstage.* PROPERTY GIRL *enters and removes house, then re-enters carrying long blue streamers, and stands at center, representing waterfall.*)

PRINCESS (*Entering with* SERVANT *and seeing waterfall*): Look! The water is flowing down over the rocks. What is this?

SERVANT: It is a waterfall.

PRINCESS: Tell me about it.

SERVANT (*Sadly*): I can only tell you the story for a price. If I told you the story for nothing, you would become terribly ill.

PRINCESS: What is the price?

SERVANT: Your sandals.

PRINCESS (*Taking off sandals*): Take them. (*They exchange sandals.*)

3RD STORYTELLER: Then the servant girl told the story of how the waterfall flowed down to join a big river, and how the river flowed out to join the big ocean. The princess was amazed, and she walked on through the rain forest, thinking of all she had heard. (PRINCESS *and* SERVANT *exit, followed by* PROPERTY GIRL, *who re-enters with cut-out of a palm tree.*)

PRINCESS (*Re-entering with* SERVANT; *seeing tree*): What is this?

SERVANT: It is a palm tree.

PRINCESS: Tell me about it.

SERVANT: I can only tell you the story for a price.

PRINCESS: What is the price?

SERVANT: Your headdress.

PRINCESS: Here. (*Gives headdress to* SERVANT, *who puts it on.*)

3RD STORYTELLER: Then the servant girl told the story of palm trees and many other trees, and how some bore delicious fruit and others provided wood. The princess was amazed, and she walked on through the rain forest, thinking of all she had heard. (PRINCESS *and* SERVANT *exit, followed by* PROPERTY GIRL, *who re-enters with model of a peacock.*)

PRINCESS (*Re-entering with* SERVANT): What is this beautiful creature?

SERVANT: It is a peacock.

PRINCESS: Tell me about it.

SERVANT (*Sadly*): I can only tell you the story for a price.

PRINCESS: What is the price?

SERVANT: Your royal cloak and jewels.

PRINCESS: Take them. (*Hands cloak and jewels to* SERVANT, *who puts them on.*)

3RD STORYTELLER: The servant girl told the princess all about peacocks and other animals, those that flew, those that swam, those that crawled, and those that ran. The princess was amazed, and she walked on through the rain forest, thinking of all she had heard. (PRINCESS *exits, followed by* SERVANT *and* PROPERTY GIRL, *who re-enters with cut-out of a rainbow.*)

PRINCESS (*Re-entering, followed by* SERVANT): What is that beautiful sight in the sky?

SERVANT: It is a rainbow.

PRINCESS: Tell me about it.

SERVANT: This is the greatest secret of all, so the price is the highest.

PRINCESS: What is the price?

SERVANT: You must promise never to tell that you are a princess and I am a servant girl.

PRINCESS: I agree.

3RD STORYTELLER: Then the servant girl told the story of the sun shining through the water in the sky. She told about the clouds and the storms and the white, cold powder that fell on the high mountains far to the east. The princess was amazed, and she walked on to the village, thinking of all she had heard. (PRINCESS *and* SERVANT *exit, followed by* PROPERTY GIRL, *who re-enters with Liberian house and stands it at left.* YOUNG CHIEF *enters left and stands by house.*) When the princess and the servant girl came to the village, the young chief mistook the servant girl for the princess, and he married her. (PRINCESS *and* SERVANT *enter right and cross to* YOUNG CHIEF, *who beckons to* SERVANT *to follow. They exit into house.*) The real princess was treated as a servant and had to crush cassava roots and rice all day long, but she was so kind and good that everybody loved her. (PRINCESS *pantomimes pounding roots.*) But the servant girl acted as she thought a princess should. She was selfish and cruel, and everybody disliked her. (SERVANT *struts out of house, pretends to kick* PRINCESS, *and struts around with her nose in the air.* PRINCESS *exits.*) Several years later, the father of the real princess came to the village to visit his daughter. (OLD CHIEF *enters,* SERVANT *sees him and runs to hide in house.* YOUNG CHIEF *enters and shakes hands with* OLD CHIEF.)

OLD CHIEF: Where is my daughter?

YOUNG CHIEF (*Pointing to house*): In there, and I would be most happy if you would take her away.

OLD CHIEF (*Peering into house*): That is not my daughter!

YOUNG CHIEF: That is not your daughter? (PRINCESS *enters. Seeing* OLD CHIEF, *she kneels at his feet.*)

OLD CHIEF: This is my daughter!

YOUNG CHIEF: That is your daughter? I've been deceived.

(He pulls SERVANT *out of house and shoos her off left. To* PRINCESS) You shall be my new wife. *(He enters house and* PRINCESS *follows him.)*

OLD CHIEF: Now I realize that I should have taught my daughter more about the world! I'm a wiser man than I was when I left my village. *(Taps head and exits. Curtain closes.* STORYTELLERS *exit, dancing and beating drum.)*

THE END

THE MONKEY WITHOUT A TAIL

THE MONKEY WITHOUT A TAIL

The people of the Amhara tribe live in the mountains and on the high plateaus of Ethiopia. Most of the Amhara tales are about cleverness, which the people value highly. One of their favorite characters is the trickster monkey. The story of the following play is a variation of a tale told by the Amharas. In other versions, the monkey without a tail is not kind, but steals the King's honey and replaces it with mud. He then persuades other monkeys to cut off their tails so they will look like him and he won't be recognized as the thief.

The Monkey Without a Tail

An Ethiopian story

Characters

STORYTELLER
PALACE ATTENDANT
RAS WAKA, *a poor man*
MEJ, *his mule*
MONKEY WITHOUT A TAIL
KING OF SHOA
QUEEN OF SHOA
SUBJECTS, *extras*

SCENE 1

BEFORE RISE: STORYTELLER *enters before curtain and crosses center.*

STORYTELLER: Many, many years ago in the high African country of Ethiopia there lived a poor man by the name of Ras Waka who had a mule called Mej. (PALACE ATTENDANT *rushes in, talking nervously.*)

PALACE ATTENDANT (*To himself; ad lib*): The best. It must be the best. Yes, yes. (*Etc.*)

STORYTELLER: Excuse me. (*They bow.*) Who are you, and why are you so nervous?

ATTENDANT (*Breathlessly*): I am the palace attendant for the King of Shoa, and he always wants something for his Queen, and I must rush around to see that it's found,

59

and you can't imagine how nerve-wracking my life is.
(*Wipes forehead*)

STORYTELLER: What does the King want this time?

ATTENDANT: The finest honey in the world. I hurry to tell
his subjects.

STORYTELLER: They are to search for the honey, are they?

ATTENDANT: Yes, and, oh, the kingdom is falling apart because the King makes incessant demands. Farmers leave
their fields, blacksmiths leave their metal, and merchants leave their shops to join the search. This time
there is a two-week deadline and a fortune waiting for
the winner. Everyone will give up everything to hunt
for the best honey. And if nobody finds it—oh, oh, I
tremble to think of the King's wrath. (*Exits, running*)

STORYTELLER: Poor Ras Waka will certainly join the
honey hunt, for he has long dreamed of becoming rich
and retiring to a peaceful, fertile valley. (*Exits; curtain
opens*)

*   *   *

SETTING: *The forest near the Abbai River in Ethiopia.
There is a backdrop curtain with several cut-outs of
tropical trees. Left center there is a fire, with two stones
for seats by it and a large jar.*

AT RISE: MONKEY WITHOUT A TAIL *is sitting by fire.* RAS
WAKA *enters right, leading* MEJ, *who has a jar tied on
back.* MEJ *is balky, wanting to rest.* MONKEY, *seeing
them coming, hides behind trees to listen.*

RAS WAKA: Come along, Mej, please. You want to sit
down every ten minutes. At this rate we'll never reach
the palace by tomorrow's deadline. (MEJ *brays in protest.* RAS WAKA *shrugs and sighs.*) All right, we'll find
a place to camp. It's almost evening, anyway. (MEJ *kicks
up heels and brays happily.* MONKEY *sneaks closer to
hear* MEJ *speak while* RAS WAKA *looks about for
campsite.*)

MEJ (*To audience*): My back aches awfully; my hooves hurt horribly. For two weeks we've been tramping through the forest near the Abbai River, hunting from village to village. Poor Ras Waka wants to win the fortune from the King of Shoa, but I don't think he, or anyone, will find the best honey in the world. And I fear everyone who fails will be punished by that selfish ruler.

MONKEY (*To audience*): Hm-m-m. The King of Shoa wants the best honey. I have a jar of honey. (*Pointing to jar near fire*) This gives me an idea for a trick. You see, a monkey without a tail, like me (*Pointing*), has a great disadvantage in the forest. Ever since I lost my tail to a lion, I have had to grow clever in order to survive. Now tricks have become my trade.

RAS WAKA: Ah, a fire ahead. I shall ask to share the campsite. (MONKEY *scurries to fire and sits as* RAS WAKA *and* MEJ *cross to fire.*)

MONKEY: Welcome to my humble fire, Ras Waka. (*Rises and bows.* RAS WAKA *returns bow.*)

RAS WAKA: Thank you, Monkey. But how is it you know my name?

MONKEY: The Monkey Without a Tail knows much about more.

RAS WAKA (*Observing* MONKEY): No tail. How interesting! (MEJ *brays, tapping* RAS WAKA *with hoof.*) Yes, Mej, I'll take that jar of honey off your back. (*Unloads jar to* MEJ's *great relief*)

MONKEY (*Feigning surprise*): You carry nothing but a jar of honey. Can that be true?

RAS WAKA (*Nodding*): Yes. I've been looking for fine honey for many days. At each village each chief told me he had the best. I kept trading one jar for another, giving up a few of my possessions with each trade. This is my seventh and last jar, since I have no more possessions and no more time to look.

MONKEY: Now you think you have the finest honey, do you?

RAS WAKA (*Shrugging*): May the water of Tisisat Falls cover my head if I know. (*They sit.* MEJ *grazes quietly.*) To tell the truth, Monkey, all honey tastes the same to me. That's my problem. I don't know how the best honey should taste.

MONKEY: Nobody does. However, I can help you.

RAS WAKA: In what way?

MONKEY: I own the finest honey in the world. (*Points to his jar.* MEJ *crosses to jar and sniffs it.*)

RAS WAKA (*Rising; excitedly*): Wonderful! Then I will give you my jar for yours, and also—(*Sighs and sits, dejectedly*) I forgot I have no possessions left, and so far no one has agreed to an even trade.

MONKEY: Never mind. You can have my jar of honey for nothing.

RAS WAKA: For nothing?

MONKEY: I will be rewarded in other ways. Even the King's fortune would do little good for a monkey in the forest.

RAS WAKA: You also know about the fortune. Is that right?

MONKEY: Yes.

RAS WAKA: Your knowledge impresses me. What makes you so sure you have the finest honey in the world?

MONKEY: I will only tell you that if I accompany you to the Palace with this jar of honey and speak to the King and Queen, they will definitely say my honey is the best. (MEJ *peers inside jar, scratching head with hoof.*)

RAS WAKA (*Rising, speaking to audience*): It seems strange to take the advice of a monkey. Yet this one seems very wise. (*To* MONKEY) All right, Monkey. In the morning we will take your honey jar to the palace. (MONKEY *and* RAS WAKA *perform a friendship ritual: they bow low to each other, then each leans over the other's right shoulder, then left shoulder and each touches ground with right hand, and finally brings hand to lips.*)

MEJ (*To audience*): My master is now friend to a monkey. That's enough to uncurl a python. (*Brays as curtain closes*)

* * * * *

SCENE 2

BEFORE RISE: STORYTELLER *enters before curtain and crosses center.*

STORYTELLER: When Ras Waka, his mule, and the Monkey Without a Tail arrived at the palace, other subjects had already gathered with their honey jars. (*Exits. Curtain opens.*)

* * *

SETTING: *The Palace of the King of Shoa. Up center are two thrones.*

AT RISE: SUBJECTS, *each with a honey jar, stand around speaking heatedly with each other.*

SUBJECTS (*Ad lib*): My honey is better than yours. No, mine is better. I have the best. I do. (*Etc.* ATTENDANT *enters, crosses center, and raises arms.*)

ATTENDANT: Sh-h-h! Hush, hush, everybody. (SUBJECTS *grow quiet.*) It's time for your honey jars to be judged by the King. May the Spirit Zar protect us all if the King doesn't think one is the best. (*Sound of drum is heard; announcing loudly*) The King and Queen of Shoa! (*Makes sweeping gesture to left.* SUBJECTS *bow and back across stage to right of thrones where they fall to knees.* ATTENDANT *stands, bowing, left of throne.* KING *enters left in a regal manner, followed by* QUEEN. *They sit on thrones.*)

KING (*Shouting*): The honey! I want the honey! (ATTEN-DANT *indicates each* SUBJECT *in turn, and each one presents jar to* KING, *bows, and then backs away left.* KING *tastes from each jar as presented, pauses to think and frown, then shakes head and passes jar to* QUEEN, *who repeats pantomime. The same pantomime is followed until all jars are presented.* KING *rises, bellowing.*) Is this all? Are there no more honey jars?

ATTENDANT (*Exclaiming*): *Yeferas gooks!** It appears so, Your Highness.

KING (*Furiously*): It all tastes the same.

QUEEN (*Nodding*): All the same.

KING (*Pointing*): You people do nothing right.

QUEEN (*Nodding*): Nothing right.

KING (*Shaking fist*): If I don't get the best honey, everyone will have to crawl on hands and knees for two weeks. (*All move away fearfully.*)

QUEEN (*Nodding, then surprised*): Everyone?

KING (*Jumping with anger*): Yes! Where is my honey? (ATTENDANT *looks behind thrones, up in air, smiles weakly, and then shrugs.* RAS WAKA, MEJ, *carrying* MONKEY's *jar on back, and* MONKEY *enter right.*)

SUBJECTS (*Surprised; ad lib*): What is this? It's Ras Waka and his mule. Look at the monkey without a tail. (*Etc.* RAS WAKA *quickly unpacks jar and presents it to* KING, *bowing, then backs right.*)

ATTENDANT (*Looking into jar*): More honey for your Highness to judge. (KING *starts to taste honey.* MONKEY *steps forward.*)

MONKEY: Wait! Before you taste, hear my words. (*All gasp with surprise.*)

KING (*Indignantly*): This monkey without a tail cannot speak to me.

---

* This exclamation is actually the name of Ethiopia's national sport, a game similar to jousting that is played on horseback.

QUEEN: How dare a lowly monkey talk to a king!

MONKEY: I am a monkey with great powers of perception. (*Moves about waving arms in dramatic, mystical manner.* SUBJECTS *draw together fearfully.*)

SUBJECTS (*Chanting*): A monkey witch. A monkey witch.

KING (*After a moment's consideration*): You may speak, monkey witch. (*Sits*)

MONKEY (*Bowing*): This jar which Ras Waka has brought to you contains the best honey in the world. However, when you taste it, you may find little difference from the honey in other jars. Yet I assure you this honey is the best.

KING: If there is little difference in taste, how can it be the best?

MONKEY: Because it is the clearest. It is so clear you can almost see through it. And therefore it makes everything and everyone else also become clear. You will see. Taste. (KING *tastes. All wait expectantly.*) Now look at your subjects there. Do they not appear to be frightened of you?

KING: They do indeed look frightened. I never noticed that before.

MONKEY: Look at your attendant. Is he [she] not nervous?

KING: Yes. Why, yes, very nervous.

MONKEY: Look at this mule. How does he look to you?

KING: Ah, let me see. The mule looks tired and extremely sore.

MONKEY: And this man, Ras Waka. What do you see when you look at him?

KING (*Considering thoughtfully*): He is kind but poor. His eyes contain dreams of a better life. (*Tastes again*) How extraordinary! This is the clearest honey I have ever seen. I see my kingdom more clearly than ever before. This honey must be the best in the world.

QUEEN (*Tasting*): M-m-m! How delicious. I believe this *is* the best honey in the world.

KING (*Rising*): Ras Waka, I hereby declare that for bringing this honey to the palace you win the fortune. (*All cheer.*) And you, my subjects (*Walks toward them*), do not be afraid of me any longer. I can clearly see that I have been a demanding ruler. Go back to your work in peace. (SUBJECTS *and* ATTENDANT *cheer and exit.* RAS WAKA *and* MEJ *rush forward to thank* MONKEY. KING *and* QUEEN *exit left as curtain closes.* STORYTELLER *enters before curtain.*)

STORYTELLER: So Ras Waka and his mule, Mej, were no longer poor. They found a fertile valley where they lived peacefully and happily for the rest of their lives. As for the Monkey Without a Tail—(MONKEY *enters.*) Excuse me, Monkey. (*They bow.*) Where did you find that excellent honey?

MONKEY: What honey?

STORYTELLER: The best honey in the world.

MONKEY: Oh, that. It was just plain, ordinary honey. You see, the best of anything is only what your mind considers so. My cleverness made it the best.

STORYTELLER (*Smiling and nodding*): I do see. You are indeed a clever monkey.

MONKEY: That's all that interests me.

STORYTELLER: Is that why you helped poor Ras Waka win the fortune, and why you helped the selfish King become a better ruler?

MONKEY: Of course. (*Glancing about to make sure no one is listening.*) Well, maybe I also like to bring happiness to others, but don't tell that to any forest creature or my reputation will be ruined. (*Exits, screeching and jumping in monkey fashion*)

STORYTELLER: So that, my friends, is the way of the Monkey Without a Tail. Peace be unto you. (*Bows and exits quickly through center curtain.*)

THE END

BATA'S LESSONS

BATA'S LESSONS

More than 3000 years ago in ancient Egypt, Ana the scribe wrote a story called, "The Tale of the Two Brothers," on which this play is based. It expresses in mythological terms the common concern about death in ancient Egypt, where the people spent much of their lives preparing for the next world.

Among the complicated beliefs held by the Egyptians in those days was the idea that each person had a Ka, a physical entity associated with the body, and a Ba or soul, an invisible entity which left the human body on death but could return in different forms after death.

In "Bata's Lessons," Ra, Ament, Isis, and Khnum represent the vast number of gods and goddesses in ancient Egyptian mythology. Almost every aspect of nature, every animal, every profession, and every milestone (such as birth, marriage, and death) had its special deities. Even the pharaohs who ruled ancient Egypt were considered to be sun-gods, and certain deities associated with them were popular during their reigns. These deities are not worshipped in modern Egypt. Since 640 A.D., when Egypt was invaded by Muslims, the religion has been that of Islam.

Bata's Lessons

A tale from ancient Egypt

Characters

NARRATOR
PALM TREE
BATA
ANPU, *his brother*
KHNUM, *god of the Nile*
ACACIA TREE
RA, *the sun-god*
AMENT, *goddess of the dead*
ISIS, *eternal mother goddess*
LOTUS, *Bata's wife*
PHARAOH
TWO SOLDIERS

SCENE 1

BEFORE RISE: *Lights go out as voice of* NARRATOR *is heard from offstage or over microphone, filtered to sound hollow and mysterious.*

NARRATOR (*Offstage*): In ancient Egypt, when gods and goddesses walked the earth, when magic deeds were done, when souls of the dead took many forms—in ancient Egypt, when Pharaohs ruled from golden thrones, then and there lived two brothers called Bata and Anpu. (*Soft Egyptian music is heard as stage lights go on and curtain opens.*)

* * *

69

SETTING: *Ancient Egypt. There is a yellow backdrop with
a river painted on it extending from ceiling height at
right down to stage level at left, gradually widening,
then painted across and downstage as if continuing into
audience. Against backdrop at right and center are
small cardboard cut-outs of pyramids as if seen from a
distance.*

AT RISE: PALM TREE *stands up center at right of river,
holding arms curved at sides.* BATA *and* ANPU *stand on
left side of river.* BATA *has sheathed sword at waist.*
KHNUM *sits in river area of stage; he is always unseen
and unheard by mortals.*

BATA: Anpu, my brother, it is time for us to part. I go to
learn the lessons of life.

ANPU: Where will you go, Bata?

BATA (*Pointing right*): Across the River Nile, beyond that
palm tree, and over the desert to some distant valley.
There I shall rest my soul and build my new home.

ANPU: Guard your soul well, little brother. And do not
forget to send for me if you need help.

BATA: I shall. And this will be the sign telling you I am
in danger: The liquid of your drink will suddenly boil.
Goodbye, brother. (*Claps* ANPU'S *arm*)

NARRATOR (*Offstage*): That day Bata crossed the great
river, while Khnum, the ever-changing god of the Nile,
gave him safe passage. (BATA *pantomimes swimming
across river.* KHNUM *rises, arms raised in protective
gesture. After crossing,* BATA *brushes off water and
waves to* ANPU, *who waves back, then exits.*) Bata
journeyed far across the hot desert sand. (*Bell music
plays as* BATA *walks in wide circle on right side of river.
Bell music is repeated whenever desert is crossed, and
same circle is followed.*) And it came to pass that one
day Bata entered the Secret Valley of the Acacia Tree.

(ACACIA TREE *enters right, standing in classic Egyptian pose—body facing audience, feet, head, and arms facing left. Arms are bent, with right hand pointing up and held over head, and left hand pointing left at shoulder level. Music ceases as* BATA *stops beside* ACACIA.)

BATA (*Looking and gesturing*): This is a wonderfully green place. The hunting should be good, and the land appears fertile. Throughout the valley stand tall, fragrant acacia trees. In the top flower of this one, my soul shall rest. (*Pantomimes taking soul from body and placing it in right hand of* ACACIA, *who then closes hand.* BATA *yawns and stretches.*) Tonight I shall sleep well, for I have found my new home. (*Kneels, head down, eyes closed, as if asleep*)

NARRATOR (*Offstage*): Now it happened that Ra, the powerful god of the sun, also came into this valley, as did Ament, the goddess of the dead, and Isis, the eternal mother goddess. (*Music plays as* RA *enters left and walks across river to center, bowing to* KHNUM, *who bows back.* AMENT *and* ISIS *enter right, dancing around* ACACIA *and* BATA. *At end of dance, music ceases, and* AMENT *and* ISIS *pose on either side of* RA, *in manner described above for* ACACIA TREE.)

AMENT: Ra, why is this man (*Indicating* BATA) in our valley?

RA: He is here to learn about life, Ament.

ISIS: Then he should be protected.

RA: No, Isis. If we protect him, he will learn little.

ISIS: Then there should be a woman to share his life.

RA (*Thinking*): Hm-m-m. Yes. A wife could teach him much.

AMENT: Let us go to the Nile where the god, Khnum, molds images. (RA *nods, and the three gods cross to river. All bow.*)

RA: Khnum, create a woman to be Bata's wife.

AMENT: Make her lovely, but not perfect.

ISIS: For she must teach both the good and bad of life.

KHNUM (*Nodding solemnly*): Wait here. (*Exits left*)

NARRATOR: Then Khnum sat down before his giant potter's wheel. He took clay and fashioned it into a woman's form, the most beautiful in Egypt. (KHNUM *re-enters, leading* LOTUS, *who has head down, eyes closed, and arms hanging straight and stiff. She wears lotus flowers in hair.*)

RA (*Gesturing and blowing*): I breathe life into her. She shall be called Lotus, born of water and daughter to the sun. (LOTUS *raises head, coming alive.* AMENT, ISIS, KHNUM, *and* RA *gesture toward* BATA. LOTUS *crosses desert. When she reaches* BATA, *he rises and moves in a nine-step circle, followed by* LOTUS. *Then they reverse direction, making another nine-step circle. Meanwhile,* AMENT *and* ISIS *exit right, dancing, and* RA *exits left, exchanging bows with* KHNUM *as he crosses river.* KHNUM *sits as before.*)

NARRATOR (*Offstage*): For many years Bata and Lotus worked hard in the valley. (BATA *and* LOTUS *pantomime tilling soil.*) They prospered and were happy together. But one night (BATA *and* LOTUS *kneel in sleeping position as before*), at a time when the moon was dark and most of the gods and goddesses were walking in another land, Bata had a frightening dream. (BATA *wakes with a cry.*)

BATA (*Shouting*): No, no!

LOTUS: What is wrong, husband?

BATA (*Rising*): I dreamed my soul's tree (*Gestures toward* ACACIA) was cut down.

LOTUS: Your soul's tree?

BATA: Yes, it is a secret I have kept from you.

LOTUS (*Jumping up*): All the time, your soul was hiding here in this tree, and I never knew. (*Examines* ACACIA) Why would it be cut down?

BATA: I do not know. However, in my dream there were swords crossing the River Nile.

LOTUS: The River Nile? What is that?

BATA: A mighty blue stream of water giving life to Egypt. It flows far to the east.

LOTUS (*Staring left*): I would like to see this mighty stream.

BATA: No, Lotus. Stay here where we both are safe. I have a feeling it is dangerous to leave our valley. (*Glancing at sky left*) But now the day dawns, and I shall go hunting. We will forget my bad dream. (*Exits right.* LOTUS *moves up and down stage on tiptoe, trying to see into left distance. Meanwhile,* NARRATOR *speaks.*)

NARRATOR (*Offstage*): Lotus grew more curious about the River Nile. Somehow, at some time, she knew she had been there—so long ago, though, she could scarcely remember.

LOTUS: If only I could see the river—just once. Then I would hurry back home. (*Looks right to make sure* BATA *is not coming*) Surely there can be no harm in looking. (*Crosses desert.* KHNUM, *astonished, leaps up, gesturing her back.*)

KHNUM: Curious woman, you do not belong here. This is a bad sign.

LOTUS (*With excitement*): It is indeed a mighty stream as my husband said. Now I remember. It was here I was born.

KHNUM: I will frighten her. Then she will return to the valley. (*Pulls flower from her hair, throwing it in river.*)

LOTUS (*Gasping and holding hair*): A flower is gone—and a lock of my hair. (*Pointing*) There it is in the river. (*Turns in alarm and starts to cross desert but hears voices off left and again grows curious*) Voices. People. I wonder who they are. Surely there can be no harm in hiding to listen. (*Hides behind* PALM. PHARAOH *enters left, followed by* TWO SOLDIERS.)

PHARAOH (*Sniffing air*): There is a rare, sweet perfume in the air. From where does it come?

1ST SOLDIER (*Pointing*): Maybe from this flower in the river, great Pharaoh. (*Hands flower to* PHARAOH, *who smells it.*)

PHARAOH: Ah-h-h, yes. (*Examining it*) See here, a strand of fine, golden hair is attached. I am enchanted. Where is this woman whose hair shines like the sun?

2ND SOLDIER (*Pointing to* PALM): I believe a woman hides behind the palm tree. There, beyond the river. (LOTUS *peeks out.*)

PHARAOH: Yes, yes, a beautiful woman! Bring her here at once. (SOLDIERS *pantomime swimming across river.* LOTUS *backs away with fear.*)

KHNUM (*Disturbed*): I shall raise a wild storm so Lotus can escape. (*Waves arms and blows.* SOLDIERS *struggle, flounder, and fall to knees.* LOTUS *crosses desert, running, and collapses near* ACACIA.)

1ST SOLDIER (*Shouting*): Help, help!

2ND SOLDIER (*Shouting*): We will drown. Help! (KHNUM, *seeing* LOTUS *safe, stops, smiles, and nods with satisfaction.* SOLDIERS *crawl to right of river, then struggle to feet, gasping, brushing off water, leaning on each other in exhaustion.*)

PHARAOH (*Shouting*): Soldiers, I command you to follow that woman. Do not return to the palace unless you bring her back. (*Exits left.* SOLDIERS *pull themselves together, then cross desert, swords drawn.* KHNUM *sighs sadly, shakes head, and sits.*)

NARRATOR (*Offstage*): For many days Pharaoh's soldiers searched through the desert. At last they came to the Secret Valley of the Acacia. And there they found Lotus. (LOTUS, *seeing* SOLDIERS *approach, rises.*)

LOTUS (*Screaming*): Bata, Bata! (BATA *re-enters, sword drawn, and has fierce battle with* SOLDIERS, *while* LOTUS *watches in fear.* 1ST SOLDIER *collapses beside* ACACIA, *clutching shoulder.* BATA *continues driving* 2ND SOLDIER *left center.* 1ST SOLDIER *pulls himself to feet by holding onto left branch (arm) of* ACACIA, *bending it with his weight. Seeing this,* LOTUS *tries to push* 1ST SOLDIER *from tree.)* Get away! Do not touch this tree. My husband's soul is hidden here. Go, go! (1ST SOLDIER *shoves* LOTUS *away. She falls. He pantomimes chopping* ACACIA *down with sword.)*

1ST SOLDIER (*Loudly*): If your husband's soul is here, then when the tree is felled, he too will die. (ACACIA *groans, sways, and opening hand above head, falls. At same time,* BATA *groans, sways, and also falls.* LOTUS *rushes to* BATA, *kneeling beside him.)*

LOTUS: Oh, Bata, my husband. (*Weeps.* ANPU *re-enters left with goblet in hand and starts to drink.)*

ANPU (*Staring into goblet*): What is this? My drink boils. My brother Bata is in danger. I must go at once to help him. (*All freeze as curtain closes.)*

* * * * *

SCENE 2

BEFORE RISE: *Stage lights go out while* NARRATOR *speaks from offstage, as* LOTUS, *wearing crown, and* SOLDIERS *enter right, unseen by audience, before curtain.*

NARRATOR (*Offstage*): And the soldiers took with them Lotus, she who was born of water and daughter to the sun. When she stood before Pharaoh, he offered her precious jewels and gold, and exquisite robes of linen and silk. (*Lights come on before curtain area, revealing stylized Egyptian tableau of* LOTUS, *haughty and demanding, and* SOLDIERS, *cowering at her feet.)* Lotus became the chief of Pharaoh's wives, the most honored Princess of Egypt. With all her new riches and power, she soon forgot Bata. But Anpu did not. (*Blackout. All exit.* NARRATOR *continues speaking as, unseen by audience,* ANPU *enters right and kneels;* ISIS *and* AMENT *enter through center curtain, and* RA *enters left.*) He journeyed to the Secret Valley of the Acacia and there wept bitterly over his brother's death. That night he had a strange dream. (*Lights come up, revealing* ANPU *in sleeping position.* AMENT, ISIS, *and* RA *cross to him.*)

AMENT: Anpu, listen well to our words. Take a seed from the fallen acacia tree. Cover that seed with water. Then your brother will live again.

RA: Although living, he will not be in human form. Instead, Bata will become the sacred bull of Ptah.

ISIS: Therefore, Anpu, if your drink should boil again, it is to the sacred bull you must go. (*Blackout. All exit. Curtain opens, and stage lights go on.*)

* * *

SETTING: *Outside Pharaoh's palace. Two folding screens are at center, angled to represent corner of palace and placed so they encompass most of river area on stage floor. Left exit leads into palace. Right exit leads into city.*

AT RISE: PALM TREE *stands beside palace corner.* LOTUS *is center, scolding* 1ST SOLDIER, *who kneels right of her, bowing profusely.*

LOTUS (*Angrily*): I told you to have the best wine sent from the noble's vineyards. What arrived this morning was disgraceful. Poor wine will never be served at palace feasts.

1ST SOLDIER (*Shaking head*): Great Princess Lotus, the noble assured me this was his best.

LOTUS: Well, it is *not* the best. Go back and tell that stupid noble he had better produce superior wine or I shall have his head chopped off. (1ST SOLDIER *rises, backing right, bowing and nodding.*) And what is more,

I may have your head chopped off, too. (1st SOLDIER *gulps, feeling neck nervously.* LOTUS *turns to exit left.*) Idiots, all of them. (*Exits proudly.* 1st SOLDIER *wipes brow, crossing left to look after her.* BATA *enters right, as bull, wearing bull headdress and without sword. He is followed by* 2ND SOLDIER.)

1st SOLDIER (*Surprised*): Why has this bull entered the courtyard of the palace?

2ND SOLDIER: Indeed it is a mystery. But what a magnificent animal!

1st SOLDIER: I will inform Pharaoh. (*Exits left, running.* BATA *snorts, paws ground, and waves head like a bull.* 2ND SOLDIER *moves quickly away.* 1st SOLDIER *re-enters, indicating* BATA *to* PHARAOH, *who also enters.*)

PHARAOH: Ah-h-h! (*Examining*) There is something magical about the sudden appearance of this creature. Perhaps he is sacred. (*Commanding*) Soldiers, guard this animal well. Revere and worship him. See that daily offerings are presented to appease his spirit. (SOLDIERS *fall to knees before* BATA. PHARAOH *muses as he starts to exit left.*) This bull has come here for a reason; yet I fear that only the gods and goddesses know why. I shall keep a close watch on what happens here. (*Exits.* SOLDIERS *rise, march right, and, drawing swords, stand guard.*)

LOTUS (*Re-entering, looking* BATA *over*): So this is what Pharaoh calls the sacred bull. I believe it is nothing more than a lost animal. Most certainly I shall not worship it. Far better if it worships me. (*Laughs, stopping short as* BATA *speaks*)

BATA: Lotus, Lotus, how mighty you have grown.

LOTUS (*Backing away*): What is this? The bull speaks my name. (*To* BATA) Who are you?

BATA: So soon have you forgotten. Do all the rich and powerful forget their humble beginnings?

LOTUS: You frighten me. (PHARAOH *re-enters, unseen by others, and hides behind* PALM TREE *to listen.*)

BATA: I am Bata, your husband in another time and place.

LOTUS (*Gasping*): Bata!

BATA: You have become far too proud and haughty, Lotus.

LOTUS: But I am a princess. I—I (*Sighs sadly*)—Bata, it is not easy to be humble when one is set above others.

BATA (*Nodding*): That is the third lesson I have learned through you.

LOTUS: What were the other two?

BATA: First: Knowledge cannot be withheld from the curious.

LOTUS: You mean when I crossed the desert to see the River Nile?

BATA: Yes, and second: A secret told to one will never again be secret.

LOTUS: You mean when you told me your soul was hidden in the acacia, and I told the soldier, and—oh, Bata, forgive me. (*Kneels*)

BATA (*Touching her head*): I forgive you, Lotus.

LOTUS: What would you have me do?

PHARAOH (*Rushing forward, yelling*): You will do nothing. (*Grabs her arm.* LOTUS *struggles.* BATA *lowers head and charges at* PHARAOH, *who releases* LOTUS *and dodges* BATA's *charges, shouting.*) Soldiers, soldiers, kill this mad bull. (SOLDIERS *pantomime killing* BATA *with swords.* BATA *dies.* LOTUS *sinks to knees, head in hands. Blackout. Curtain closes. Lights come on before curtain area.* ANPU *enters through center curtain, carrying goblet.*)

ANPU: My drink boils again. (ISIS *enters right;* AMENT *enters left.*)

ISIS: Go to the palace courtyard, Anpu. There you will find your slain brother.

AMENT: Take two drops of his blood and plant them

beside the River Nile. Then your brother will live again in still another form. (*All exit. Curtain opens on river setting of Scene 1.* KHNUM *sits in river and* PALM TREE *stands to right of river as before.* BATA, *holding papyrus plant, kneels down right of river.* LOTUS *kneels in river near* BATA. *They face each other. There is no movement.*)

NARRATOR (*Offstage*): Anpu obeyed the goddesses' command. From the two drops of blood, tall papyrus grew beside the River Nile. Then Lotus prayed to the god Ra, asking to be with Bata. And it came to pass that Ra sent Lotus to live in the water near the papyrus. Even today they dwell there, the lotus and papyrus, close to each other. (*Music plays as curtain closes slowly.*)

THE END

TRICKSTER HARE'S FEAST

TRICKSTER HARE'S FEAST

In many African tales, a small, weak, but smart creature and a large, strong, but dim-witted creature start out as friends. They make a contract to do something. Everything is fine as long as the contract is obeyed by both parties. Inevitably, however, the large creature breaks the contract, placing the small creature in danger. At that point, cleverness must be used if the little animal is to survive.

How prominent these trickster stories are in a particular culture seems to reflect how dangerous that culture considers the world about them. Where life is hard, where people must struggle to survive, and especially where colonial rule has oppressed the people, trickster tales abound. Thus, through lore, African children learn the importance of using their wits as well as their physical skills to stay alive and get ahead in the world.

Trickster Hare's Feast

A tale from Uganda

Characters

ELEPHANT
HARE
KAGWA, *a merchant*
NAMBI, *his wife*
THREE MERCHANTS
THREE WASHER WOMEN
HYENA
LEOPARD
LION

SCENE 1

BEFORE RISE: ELEPHANT *and* HARE *enter at rear of auditorium and come down aisle toward stage. Each carries a folded bundle of cloth.*

ELEPHANT: All right, Hare. We are true partners.

HARE: Yes, Elephant. We shall share everything.

ELEPHANT: First we will go to the marketplace with our two bundles of cloth.

HARE (*Nodding*): Yes. We will trade the cloth for as many chickens as we can.

ELEPHANT (*Nodding*): And then we will go to your compound and have a big feast.

HARE: Sharing everything—fifty-fifty.

83

ELEPHANT: Of course. (*Points to area below stage*) Here we are at the river.

HARE: It's very deep. Let me ride on your back, Elephant, while you wade across.

ELEPHANT: What? Don't be foolish. Follow me. (*Pantomimes wading to stage steps*) See? The water only comes up to my knees.

HARE: I am smaller than you are, and it will come up to my nose!

ELEPHANT (*Climbing to stage*): Too bad, friend Hare. (*Snickers*) I don't want to get wet again. You'll have to cross by yourself.

HARE: See here, Elephant, partners should share their problems as well as their rewards.

ELEPHANT (*Taunting*): Why are you upset about a little thing like crossing the river by yourself? (*Laughs*) Are you afraid?

HARE: No, but I am not very good at swimming. (*Angrily*) This is not very considerate of you to make me swim across! (*Pantomimes jumping into river and swimming awkwardly, gasping, trying to hold cloth out of water.* HARE *finally reaches stairs, breathless, then shakes off water and sits, exhausted.*)

ELEPHANT (*Laughing and pointing*): Your cloth is all wet and muddy. (HARE *pantomimes squeezing water from cloth.*)

HARE: It wouldn't be if you had helped me.

ELEPHANT: I'll bet I can get more chickens for my clean cloth than you can for your dirty cloth. So, why should I share with you anymore? I will not be your partner any longer!

HARE (*Rising in indignation*): What?

ELEPHANT: Farewell, Hare. (*Exits right*)

HARE (*Crossing arms indignantly*): What an ungrateful

fellow! (*Scratches head thoughtfully*) I shall see if I can teach the Elephant a lesson. I'm not called the trickster for nothing! (*Curtain opens as* HARE *exits right.*)

* * *

SETTING: *Marketplace near a village in Uganda, under a shady umbrella tree. Center is sawhorse frame with four plump chickens and one skinny chicken hanging on it.*

AT RISE: MERCHANTS *are arranging their wares—cooking pots, knives, sweet potatoes, plantains—on colorful cloths.* KAGWA *and* NAMBI *stand at frame, center.* WASHER WOMEN *enter, holding bundles of clothing on their heads. They stop to buy some food.*

1ST MERCHANT: Fresh plantains.

2ND MERCHANT: My cooking pots are sturdy.

3RD MERCHANT: Large, sweet potatoes.

KAGWA: Delicious chickens.

1ST WASHER WOMAN (*To* 1ST MERCHANT): Your price for plantains is too high.

2ND WASHER WOMAN (*To* 2ND MERCHANT): I will give you a knife for two cooking pots.

3RD WASHER WOMAN: That seems fair.

ELEPHANT (*Entering, carrying folded cloth*): All right! All right! (*Stamping and bellowing*) Stop everything this instant. I am here to trade cloth for chickens. Quiet! (*Others whisper to each other in surprise.* ELEPHANT *shouts at* WASHER WOMEN.) Silly women! Get out of my way. (*WASHER WOMEN stand, hands on hips, angrily staring at him. He crosses to* KAGWA.) Hello there, Kagwa. Give me your five chickens for this cloth. (*Holds out cloth*)

KAGWA: No! Not so fast, friend Elephant. My chickens are worth a great deal more than your thin cloth.

ELEPHANT: How dare you refuse! Why, I'll just take the chickens, then.

KAGWA (*Rising*): These chickens belong to Nambi and me. If you touch any of them, I will call out, "Thief!" and everyone in the marketplace will go after you.

ELEPHANT (*Looking about in surprise*): What's that you say?

MERCHANTS (*Nodding and murmuring assent, ad lib*): That is right. That's what we'll do. (*Etc.*)

ELEPHANT: Listen, Kagwa, this cloth of mine is very fine. (*Holding up cloth*) You had better trade the chickens for it. (NAMBI *starts to examine cloth.* ELEPHANT *bellows.*) Keep your hands off my cloth!

NAMBI (*With haughty disdain*): You are very rude.

KAGWA (*Indicating skinny chicken*): This scrawny chicken is all I will give in exchange for your skimpy cloth.

ELEPHANT: Ridiculous! The cloth is worth much more.

KAGWA: Take it, or go away with no chicken at all.

ELEPHANT: One skinny chicken for my beautiful cloth. That's not fair.

KAGWA: No, it is only because I am a generous man that I offer you anything at all. You would get nothing from the other merchants. (*Gives him skinny chicken and takes cloth*) Now, go on your way, and give the other customers a chance to buy. (*Turns away. Selling resumes in pantomime between* MERCHANTS *and* WASHER WOMEN. ELEPHANT *takes chicken and crosses right, just as* HARE *enters at right, with cloth.*)

ELEPHANT (*To* HARE): You won't have any luck here. That merchant called Kagwa would trade only this bony chicken for my fine cloth. (*Holds up chicken*)

HARE (*Pretending sympathy*): What a shame!

ELEPHANT: I shall sit under the acacia tree and glare at him. (ELEPHANT *stamps off right.* HARE *watches him go, then crosses to* KAGWA.)

HARE: Good day to you, Kagwa. Is this your charming wife?

KAGWA (*Smiling*): Yes, this is Nambi.

HARE: My, what a lucky man you are to be married to such a beautiful woman. (NAMBI *giggles*.)

NAMBI (*Beaming*): Thank you, kind Hare.

HARE: Look at these marvelous chickens! You must raise the finest chickens in all Uganda.

KAGWA: I try my best.

HARE: You certainly do! Now, I have here a bundle of cloth. It is slightly wet and soiled from crossing the river, but when it is dry, the dirt can be brushed away easily. (*Opens cloth and displays it*) Wouldn't this make a beautiful dress for your lovely wife?

KAGWA: Perhaps it would.

HARE: When Nambi wears a dress made from this cloth, everyone will look at her and say, "There goes a woman dressed in the finest cloth. Her husband must be wealthy."

NAMBI (*Handling cloth*): The pattern is pretty, Kagwa.

KAGWA: Do you like it, Nambi?

NAMBI: Very much.

HARE: I am willing to part with this excellent cloth for only five chickens.

KAGWA: I have only four chickens left.

HARE: Hm-m-m. You are such kind people that I will let the cloth go for four chickens, then.

KAGWA: Agreed. (*Exchanges chickens for cloth.* NAMBI, *smiling, drapes the cloth around herself and* WASHER WOMEN *cross to admire it.*)

HARE: Thank you. Good day to you both. (*Bows and exits right.* MERCHANTS *resume selling as curtain closes.*)

* * * * *

Scene 2

Before Rise: Elephant *enters left and* Hare *enters right in front of curtain,* Elephant *carrying his scrawny chicken and* Hare *with his four fat chickens.*

Elephant: Why, hello! Look at that! You did very well, partner. Our five chickens will make a fine feast.

Hare: Wait a minute. You said you didn't want to be partners anymore. Now, because I have four plump chickens, you suddenly want to be partners again. Well, forget it. Go and eat your scrawny chicken by yourself. I am going down to the stream now (*Points off right*), and then I am going to my compound to have a fine feast, just for myself. (*Exits right.* Elephant *stamps.*)

Elephant (*Bellowing after him*): Selfish creature! Go ahead and eat your chickens yourself! I don't want to eat anything of yours anyway! (*Turns away as* Hyena *enters left*)

Hyena: Don't move! (Elephant *trumpets in alarm.*) Give me that chicken you have or I'll bite you. (*Snaps jaws*)

Elephant (*Trembling*): Hyena, you don't want my tiny chicken. (*Points off right*) Soon, Hare will be here, and he has four fat chickens.

Hyena: That sounds delicious. Move on before I change my mind. (*Sits and stares off right.* Elephant *quickly crosses to center. Suddenly,* Leopard *leaps on at left and confronts* Elephant, *who trumpets in alarm again.*)

Leopard: I am very hungry. I would like to eat something—maybe an elephant.

Elephant: I would surely give you indigestion, Leopard. Look (*Points off right*)—young, tender Hare will be coming this way soon, and he has four fat chickens.

Leopard: Marvelous! In that case, go on your way. (Leopard *crouches at center, staring off right.* Elephant *quickly crosses left.* LION *enters left, roaring.*)

LION: I am starved. I will eat anything—even your long trunk and floppy ears, Elephant.

ELEPHANT: Lion, there is no need to waste your time with me. I know where you can get a good meal. (*Points right*) Hare will be coming down this path soon with four fat chickens.

LION: M-m-m, then I won't bother to eat you. You would probably be leathery, anyway. (LION *crouches and stares right.* ELEPHANT *sighs with relief.*)

ELEPHANT (*To himself*): The Hare won't have his feast, after all. This will be the end of him, and I am not one bit sorry. (*Laughs, then exits left.* HARE *reenters, still carrying chickens.* HYENA *grabs one of his arms.*)

HYENA: Give me those chickens!

HARE: Why, hello there, Hyena. (*Nervously*) I—uh—I can't give you these chickens because they are for—uh—a feast that I am going to give.

HYENA: That is not a good enough reason.

HARE: You don't understand. The feast is being held by—uh—the great Mugassa.

HYENA: The great Mugassa? Who is that?

HARE: The powerful spirit of the forest. He is extremely dangerous.

HYENA: I don't believe you.

HARE: Mugassa is waiting for these chickens and he will be in a rage if I don't hurry. (*Starts left*)

HYENA: Wait! This feast of the great Mugassa—(*Suspiciously*) who is going to be there?

HARE: I understand you are going to be invited, Hyena.

HYENA: Then what are we doing here? Let us go to your compound at once. (HARE *crosses right and* HYENA *follows. As they reach center,* LEOPARD *snarls and grabs* HARE's *arm.*)

LEOPARD: Those chickens will be my dinner.

HARE: Hello there, Leopard. I'm taking these chickens to the feast of the great Mugassa.

HYENA: Yes. He is the powerful and dangerous spirit of the forest.

HARE: He is giving a feast at my compound, and the Hyena is a guest. You are invited, too.

LEOPARD: I will be happy to attend. (HARE *again crosses right, followed by* HYENA *and* LEOPARD. *As they go right,* LION *roars and grabs* HARE'S *arm.*)

HARE: Hello there, Lion. You must be waiting for us. I'm taking these chickens to the feast of the great Mugassa.

HYENA: He is the powerful and dangerous spirit of the forest.

LEOPARD: He is giving a feast at the Hare's compound.

HARE: You are invited, too.

LION: Let us go at once. (*Follows* LEOPARD, *who follows* HYENA, *who follows* HARE. *All exit left. Curtain opens.*)

* * *

SETTING: *Inside Hare's compound. Up left is large double gate with closing bar. Gate is open. Right center is cardboard cutout of thatched house. Doorway is covered with hanging cloth. In front of house is a drum. Kettle, ax, and knife are upstage.*

AT RISE: HARE *enters, still carrying chickens, leading* HYENA, LEOPARD *and* LION. *He puts chickens down beside drum.*

HARE: Wait here. I shall go into the house to ask ·the great Mugassa what he wants us to do. (*Enters house*)

HYENA (*To others*): Do you know anything about the great Mugassa?

LION: I think I have heard that he is quick to anger.

LEOPARD: I believe I have heard that his face is terrifying to see.

HYENA: We'd better be on good behavior so we won't make him angry. (*Others nod.* HARE *comes out of house, gets kettle, ax and knife, and crosses to where others are standing.*)

HARE: The great Mugassa insists that everyone must have an equal share. The Lion must fill the kettle with water, so that we can start to cook the chickens. (LION *takes kettle.*) Leopard is to chop wood for the fire to heat the water. (LEOPARD *takes ax.*) Hyena is to cut some big banana leaves for plates. (HYENA *takes knife.*)

HYENA: What are you supposed to do, Hare?

HARE: Guard the chickens. It is very important. If something should happen to them, the great Mugassa would be furious with us! His wrath is more deadly than a thousand spears tipped with poison. (*Others look at each other, then nod.*) The sooner we finish, the sooner we eat. (*Others exit hurriedly through gate. To himself*) Whew! I have to keep one step ahead of them. Let me see. . . . Hm-m-m . . . (*Suddenly*) I have it! I shall take a leg from one of these chickens, and hide it in my house. (*Takes leg from chicken*) My drum will also be useful. (*Gets drum and takes it into house, along with chicken leg, then comes out again*)

LION (*Reentering; carrying kettle with effort, as if it is very heavy*): I have filled the kettle with water, Hare. (LEOPARD *and* HYENA *follow him in.*)

LEOPARD (*Carrying ax and load of wood*): And here is the wood for the fire.

HYENA (*Carrying five banana leaves and knife*): I found five large banana leaves.

HARE: You are all back so soon! Excellent! (*Others put kettle, leaves, and wood down center stage.*) Now, to cook the feast. (*Examining each chicken*) This one is all right. This one is fine, too. And so is this one. (*In mock alarm*) Oh, no! Something is wrong with this chicken!

LION: What is wrong?

HARE: The leg is missing. (*Displays chicken. Others gasp in horror and look at each other nervously.*)

HYENA: I didn't take it.

LEOPARD: Nor did I. (LEOPARD *and* HYENA *look accusingly at* LION.)

LION: Why are you looking at me? I am not guilty.

HARE: The great Mugassa will be angry.

HYENA: What will he do?

HARE: I fear the worst. He may even destroy us.

LION: I didn't even go near the chickens. (LEOPARD *and* HYENA *stare at him.*) Well, I went no closer than you two.

HARE (*Wailing*): It was my fault! I had the job of guarding the chickens. I must confess my failure. This will be the end of all of us. (*Starts toward house, head hanging, moving slowly*)

LEOPARD: Wait a minute.

HYENA: Don't go in there.

LION: Stop! (HARE *enters house.*)

LION, LEOPARD *and* HYENA (*Ad lib*): What shall we do? This is terrible. We will be destroyed. A thousand poisoned spears! (*Etc.*)

LION (*Roaring*): I didn't touch the chickens! (*From inside house, sound of drumbeat is heard. Others start to back away from house.*)

HARE (*From inside; in loud, deep voice*): I, the great Mugassa, am wild with fury! How dare you spoil one of my chickens! I shall finish you off *right now!* (*Gives bloodcurdling yell. Drumbeat gets faster. Others flee in terror, pushing each other out of the way.*)

LION, LEOPARD *and* HYENA (*Ad lib*): The great Mugassa is after us! Help! Help! (*Etc. They exit at gate.* HARE *emerges from house, carrying drum.*)

HARE (*Smiling; to audience*): Ha, ha! My plan worked.

Now I will have these four plump chickens all to myself! (HARE *strolls over to gate as* ELEPHANT *enters.*)

ELEPHANT (*Shocked*): Hare, I can't believe you escaped safely from the Hyena, Leopard and Lion! They were going to eat you.

HARE (*With amusement*): Why, Elephant, it was simple. They even helped me fill my kettle with water, chop wood for my fire, and gather banana leaves for my plates. (HARE *holds up chickens, puts them into kettle.* ELEPHANT *shakes head in disbelief.*) The biggest helper, though, was (*Beats drum; in deep, loud voice*) *the great Mugassa!* (ELEPHANT *scratches head, puzzled, and* HARE *collapses in laughter as curtain falls.*)

THE END

THE GREAT TUG OF WAR

THE GREAT TUG OF WAR

The tricksters in most African tales are small animals with large animals as their dupes. A storyteller uses the local creatures his audience knows well.

In East Africa, Hare, Mongoose, Tortoise, Chameleon, and Frog play trickster roles, Hare being the most common. Some stories speak of Hare as a male; quite often, though, Hare is a female. Dupes are mainly Hyena and Elephant, although other large, strong animals are substituted in certain areas. Always, however, the stories are lessons that demonstrate how brains can win over brawn.

An interesting version of the tug-of-war tale is told in the Cape Verde Islands off the coast of West Africa. In it, the dupes are Elephant and Whale. Near rivers in East Africa, the tale is often told with Lion and Crocodile as the dupes. In most versions one creature is from land, the other from water.

The Great Tug of War

A tale from East Africa

Characters

HARE
VULTURE
MAT MAKER ⎱ *villagers*
ELDER ⎰
BIG, OLD ELEPHANT
GIANT HIPPOPOTAMUS
TWO LORDLY LIONS

SCENE 1

SETTING: *African savanna. Village up right. Bushes left center; water hole to right of it, acacia trees to left.*

AT RISE: HARE, *asleep behind bushes, wakes up and stretches.*

HARE (*Yawning*): The sun greets the African plains. It's time for me to wake up and give greetings, too. (*Jumps from bushes and bows to each*) Good morning, water hole. Good morning, acacia trees. Good morning, tall grass. (*Looks about in horror, then shrieks with anger*) Eeeee! Where *is* the tall grass? It's gone—trampled down. Oh, no! Now I have lost my security. Nothing hides my home from the Lordly Lions. (*Sniffs air, then ground*) Ah, hah! I smell the villain—Big, Old Elephant. While I slept, he stomped down on my grass.

VULTURE (*Entering as if flying*): Was that you yelling? (*Eagerly*) Are you in trouble, Hare?

97

HARE: Yes, Vulture. Big, Old Elephant flattened down the grass around my home.

VULTURE: Is that all! So what! There's nothing in it for me. (*Exits left*)

HARE (*Yelling after him*): Well, I'm glad. Go hover over the zebras. (*Looks toward water*) I'd better calm down about my trampled grass problem. I'll hop down to the water hole for a cool drink. (*Hops over to water, stares at it, then shrieks in anger*) Eeeee! The water hole is a muddy mess. I can't drink this dirty stuff. (*Examines footprints*) Ah, hah! I recognize the villain's footprints—Giant Hippopotamus. While I slept, she lumbered over from the river and wallowed in my water hole.

VULTURE (*Reentering*): Was that you yelling again? (*Eagerly*) Are you in bigger trouble, Hare?

HARE: Yes! Giant Hippopotamus muddied up my water hole.

VULTURE: Is that all! So what! There's nothing in it for me.

HARE: Buzz away, you beady-eyed Vulture. You make me nervous.

VULTURE: Hmpf! You're no help to a hungry bird. (*Exits*)

HARE (*Calling after him*): Good! (*Scratches ears*) I'd better hop over to the village and talk to the people. Surely, they will know how to deal with naughty animals who ruin property. I hope they'll send out a delegation to scold them. (*Hops to village and calls*) Hello! Anybody home? (MAT MAKER *enters up right center, carrying mat.*)

MAT MAKER: Good day, Hare. Most villagers are out herding cattle. (*Unrolls mat and sits on it*) Can I help you?

HARE (*Sitting on ground*): I hope so, kind mat maker. I want to tell you about the awful thing Big, Old Elephant did.

MAT MAKER (*Raising arms; in wonder*): Big, Old Elephant is such a mighty creature. His trunk can uproot trees; his tusks can split open a rock; and his hide is as tough as a coconut shell. Since Big, Old Elephant is one of the strongest creatures in the world, he can do no wrong.

HARE: Really? He can do *no* wrong?

MAT MAKER: That's right. Now, what did you wish to tell me?

HARE (*Rising*): Never mind. Is there a wise elder left in the village?

MAT MAKER (*Rising, rolling up mat*): Yes. Our wisest elder seldom goes anyplace these days.

HARE: May I speak with him, please?

MAT MAKER: I'll see if he is available to meet with you. (*Exits into village*)

HARE: Surely, a wise elder will help a poor, little creature solve its problems. (ELDER *enters from village, pipe in mouth and carrying stool.*)

ELDER: Good day, Hare. (HARE *bows;* ELDER *sits on stool and gestures for her to be seated;* HARE *sits on ground.*) You wish to discuss something?

HARE (*Nodding*): I want to tell you about the awful thing Giant Hippopotamus did.

ELDER: Ah-h-h-h! (*Pantomimes puffing on pipe*) I have great admiration for Giant Hippopotamus because of her tremendous strength. Have you heard the story about how she tied two giraffe necks together into a knot?

HARE: No, I hadn't heard that one.

ELDER: Then, there's the tale about how she spanked a pride of lions because their roars woke her up. (*Chuckling*) It would be foolish ever to interfere with Giant Hippopotamus.

HARE (*Rising*): I see.

ELDER: Now, what did you wish to tell me?

HARE: Never mind. (*Bows*) Excuse me. I have important work to do. (*Hops back to bushes while* ELDER *shrugs, rises and exits with stool into village.* HARE *addresses audience.*) Obviously, I must solve my problems by myself. (*Thinks a moment, then snaps fingers*) I know what to do. (*Hops left to acacia trees and shouts*) Hey, Big, Old Elephant, you're not as strong as you think you are.

ELEPHANT (*Entering left, stamping in fury*): Nobody insults me. Who said that?

HARE: I did.

ELEPHANT: You? Insignificant, puny, little Hare?

HARE: No! Powerful Hare.

ELEPHANT (*Laughing*): Is that a joke?

HARE: It's no joke. I'm stronger than you are, and to prove it I challenge you to a tug of war.

ELEPHANT: That's the funniest thing since I forced a troop of monkeys to sit on an ant hill.

HARE: You may think it's funny, but I'm quite serious. Tomorrow at sunrise, our great tug of war begins. What's more, there will be witnesses, so you'd better meet me.

ELEPHANT: Where?

HARE (*Pointing to acacias*): Behind those trees. See you in the morning. (*Hops right*)

ELEPHANT (*To audience*): That poor, silly creature doesn't have a chance. (*Exits left, laughing*)

HARE (*Shouting off right*): Hey, Giant Hippopotamus, swimming in the river, you're not as strong as you think you are.

HIPPOPOTAMUS (*Entering right, grunting furiously*): Nobody insults me. Who said that?

HARE: I did.

HIPPOPOTAMUS: You? Tiny, feeble hare?

HARE: No! Powerful Hare.

HIPPOPOTAMUS (*Giggling*): Don't be a silly pipsqueak.

HARE: I'm not a silly pipsqueak. I'm stronger than you are. To prove it, I challenge you to a tug of war.

HIPPOPOTAMUS (*Giggling again*): That's the funniest thing since I tossed a crocodile onto the thorns of an acacia tree.

HARE: You may think it's funny, but I'm quite serious. Tomorrow at sunrise our great tug of war begins. What's more, there will be witnesses, so you'd better meet me.

HIPPOPOTAMUS: Where?

HARE (*Pointing*): Here at the water hole. See you in the morning. (*Hops down center*)

HIPPOPOTAMUS (*To audience*): That silly Hare is too ridiculous for words. (*Exits right, giggling*)

HARE: Now I shall return to the village to invite the mat maker and the elder to witness the great struggle in the morning. (*Gets an idea and raises a paw*) Also, I shall go to the home of the Lordly Lions, and invite them, too. (*Gets another idea and raises other paw*) And, I shall invite that miserable Vulture. (*Claps paws*) Then, I shall make a long, strong rope. (*Rolls eyes and hops into air*) I can hardly wait to demonstrate my fantastic strength to everyone. (*Blackout; curtain*)

*   *   *   *   *

SCENE 2

TIME: *Next morning at sunrise.*

SETTING: *Same.*

AT RISE: HARE, *with rope, hides behind bushes.* LORDLY LIONS *enter, roaring, followed by* VULTURE, *flapping wings and croaking.*

1ST LORDLY LION: Strange that Hare should invite us to

watch his defeat. This should be an entertaining morning.

2ND LORDLY LION: About time someone took care of that insolent Hare. Afterwards, we will eat her for breakfast.

VULTURE: I'm counting on you to leave a few pickings for me.

1ST LION: We always do, you mangy bird.

2ND LION: For now, Vulture, keep your distance, and no more disgusting croaks until this tug of war is finished.

VULTURE: All right, all right. Where are we supposed to stand to witness the disaster?

1ST LION: Up near the acacia trees. That's where Hare asked us to be.

2ND LION (*Looking at village*): Here come the two village witnesses. Places, everybody. (LIONS, VULTURE *stand up left;* MAT MAKER, ELDER *enter from village and stand up right.* HARE *jumps from bushes, carrying rope, and hops left.*)

HARE (*Calling*): Are you here, Big, Old Elephant?

ELEPHANT (*Entering left*): Of course I'm here. I wouldn't miss this for anything.

HARE: This is your end of the rope. Place the loop around your body. (ELEPHANT *slips loop over body.*) I shall be in the bushes. (*Points*) The only favor I ask of you is to stay behind this acacia tree (*Indicates*) and never turn your face toward me.

ELEPHANT: That's a simple request.

HARE: Now, the game goes this way: If I am pulled from the bushes into the grass, you win; if you are pulled from the trees into the grass, you lose. The witnesses will be the judges.

ELEPHANT: Everybody knows I'm going to win.

HARE (*Slyly*): We'll see about that.

ELEPHANT: How do I know when this ridiculous tug of war is to start?

HARE: The witnesses will call out, *"Moja, mbili, vuta!"* (NOTE: Swahili for "One, two, pull!")

ELEPHANT: I understand. (*Stands behind tree, facing left*)

HARE (*Quickly hopping right and calling off*): Giant Hippopotamus.

HIPPOPOTAMUS (*Entering right*): Yes, yes, I'm here. Let's get on with this foolish game.

HARE: This is your end of the rope. Place the loop around your body. (HIPPOPOTAMUS *slips rope around her body.*) I shall be in the bushes. (*Points*) The only favor I ask is that you go into the water hole (*Indicates*) and never turn your face toward me.

HIPPOPOTAMUS: Who cares. I don't want to look at you anyway.

HARE: Now, the game goes this way: If I am pulled from the bushes into the grass, you win; if you are pulled from the water hole into the grass, you lose. The witnesses will be the judges.

HIPPOPOTAMUS: There's no question about my winning.

HARE: We'll see about that.

HIPPOPOTAMUS: How do we start the game?

HARE: The witnesses will call out, *"Moja, mbili, vuta!"*

HIPPOPOTAMUS: All right. (*Stands in water hole, facing right*) I'm ready. (*Witnesses have watched this with curiosity.* HARE *picks up center of rope and hops behind bushes.*)

HARE (*Calling*): I'm ready, witnesses.

WITNESSES (*Calling in unison*): Moja, mbili, vuta! (ELE-PHANT *and* HIPPOPOTAMUS *pull against each other, grunting and groaning, while* HARE *jumps up and down in the middle, looking left one time and right the next. Villagers smother giggles,* LIONS *look disgusted, and* VULTURE *croaks with indignation.*)

HARE (*Shouting with glee*): Can't you pull any harder than

that? What a puny weakling you are. I am much stronger than you. Why, I'm using only one paw, and I'm not even out of breath. (ELEPHANT *gives a giant yank and* HIPPOPOTAMUS *is pulled into grass;* HIPPOPOTAMUS *snorts angrily and gives a huge yank and* ELEPHANT, *trumpeting loudly, is pulled into grass;* ELEPHANT *and* HIPPOPOTAMUS *throw off rope loops and turn to face* HARE, *who leaps from bushes to center, holding rope high, and calls to* ELDER *and* MAT MAKER.) Who won? Who won?

MAT MAKER (*Amused*): Hare won.

ELDER: No question about it.

HARE (*To other witnesses*): And what is your decision?

LIONS (*In unison, disgusted*): Unfortunately for us, Hare won.

VULTURE (*Hissing at* ELEPHANT *and* HIPPOPOTAMUS): Stupid! Stupid!

ELEPHANT (*Sadly*): I'll have to admit, Hare, your remarkable strength pulled me into the grass.

HIPPOPOTAMUS (*Astonished*): Did Hare beat you, too?

ELEPHANT: Yes. (*Frightened*) Oh, no! Hare must have pulled both of us into the grass.

HIPPOPOTAMUS: My goodness! I'm afraid he did.

ELEPHANT (*Horrified, pointing at* HARE): This animal is filled with super-creature strength. I'm getting out of here, and I won't ever come back. (*Exits left, bellowing*) Help! Help! Big, Old Hare is on the loose.

HIPPOPOTAMUS (*Backing away in terror*): Don't hurt me, please. I'll be good. I'll stay away from your water hole. (*Turns and lumbers away, exiting right, wailing*) Help! Help! Beware of the Giant Hare. (*Villagers burst into laughter and come down center to* HARE; LIONS *and* VULTURE *also come down, shaking heads in disgust.*)

1ST LION: You certainly outwitted those two strong creatures.

2ND LION: We'd better fade into the sunrise and make a meal on a creature who is not as clever as you are. (LIONS *exit right, followed by annoyed* VULTURE.)

VULTURE (*Croaking as he exits*): I got nothing out of this whole transaction. Nothing at all.

MAT MAKER: Congratulations, Hare. You've made me change my mind. Just because someone is strong, doesn't mean he is right.

ELDER: Yes. And I have revised my wisdom. Strength doesn't always win if your opponent is smarter. (*Blackout; curtain*)

THE END

MANTIS, THE DREAMER

MANTIS

The hot, dry Kalahari Desert is home to the Bushmen, the most commonly used name of the San people. They are thought to be the oldest inhabitants of southern Africa. Rarely taller than five feet, they traditionally existed as hunters and gatherers, skilled in the arts of survival. The tiniest things can produce the greatest achievements, they say, for was not the world created by the Praying Mantis, a small insect that hunts with ferocity? Interestingly, the triangular-shaped head and bright eyes of the Mantis suggest a typical Bushman face. No wonder Mantis plays such an important role in Bushmen lore.

It is Mantis who sends rain, brings good luck to hunters, and protects people from sickness and danger. Although a supernatural creature, Mantis has human traits that make him far from perfect. He is full of mischief, procrastination, and fear. Often he gets into trouble because of his shortcomings. But he learns from his mistakes, as every wise human should.

Mantis lore comprises one part of a wealth of Bushmen stories handed down over many centuries, tales that reveal the people's reverence for nature and explain how an individual fits into the design of life.

Mantis, the Dreamer

Adapted from Kalahari Bushmen tales

Characters

PRAYING MANTIS
DASSIE ROCK RABBIT, *his wife*
KWAMMANGA RAINBOW SPIRIT
MONGOOSE
LION CUB
WISE ELAND
MOTHER LION

TIME: *In the beginning, when animals and spirits were people.*
SETTING: *Kalahari Desert. Up left is a water hole, partially surrounded by bushes; down right is a grass hut.*
AT RISE: PRAYING MANTIS *stands, gazing at sky, chin cupped in hands in a dream pose;* DASSIE ROCK RABBIT, *who frequently wrinkles nose, sits in hut doorway.*

DASSIE (*Looking at* MANTIS): Mantis, my husband, there is nothing for supper. Why do you stand there gazing at the sky and dreaming? Go out and hunt for food.
MANTIS: But Dassie, my Rock Rabbit wife, my dreams are so wonderful. In this last dream I saw fresh meat waiting for us.
DASSIE (*Wryly*): Then find it and bring it back. Empty stomachs are not filled by dreams, Mantis. They are filled by action.

MANTIS: Yes, yes. That's what we need—action! (*Returns to dreaming;* KWAMMANGA RAINBOW SPIRIT *and* MONGOOSE, *carrying large bag, enter left and cross to hut.*)

KWAMMANGA: Mantis, Wise Eland just told me a pride of lions came to the water hole and killed a zebra. (MANTIS *shivers with fear.*)

MONGOOSE: He told Kwammanga (*Indicates him*) that we should go over and visit the lions.

MANTIS (*Horrified*): Visit the lions? Why?

MONGOOSE: Because Wise Eland believes the lions will give us meat . . . although he cautioned us to be careful and polite.

KWAMMANGA: So, Mongoose and I plan to follow Wise Eland's advice. Would you like to come, too?

MANTIS: Oh, well, I . . . ah—

DASSIE (*Quickly*): Yes! Mantis would love to go. Wouldn't you, dear husband? You were just dreaming about that meat.

MANTIS (*Nervously*): Ah . . . (*Clears throat*) Of course. Quite right, Dassie, my sweet Rock Rabbit wife.

MONGOOSE: If you are scared of lions, Mantis, it might be better if you stay home.

MANTIS (*With bravado*): Me, scared? No, no. Lions are my friends.

KWAMMANGA: Good. First, we will search for their tracks. Then, we will follow them to the kill. (*Crosses to water hole, hunting for tracks;* MONGOOSE *also crosses, inspecting ground;* MANTIS *doesn't move.*) Ho! (*Points at ground*) Here are the lion tracks.

DASSIE: Mantis, you still dream. Where is the action?

MANTIS: Ah, hm-m-m. (*Gulps, then, to* DASSIE, *attempting to be brave*) All right! I am off with Kwammanga and Mongoose to visit my great friends, the lions. (DASSIE *waves goodbye and exits into hut;* MANTIS *waves back, then cautiously crosses to water hole and inspects tracks.*) How do you know these are lion tracks?

KWAMMANGA: By the large size of the paws and the great length of the claws. Look. (*Indicates*) The lions leaped on the zebra right here. Then they dragged the carcass away to eat.

MANTIS (*Peering about nervously*): Maybe a lion stayed behind. Maybe it plans to leap out onto us.

KWAMMANGA: I doubt it. Still, there could be danger.

MONGOOSE: Mantis, if you are frightened, go home. (LION CUB *enters left, sniffing ground, unseen by* MANTIS.)

MANTIS (*Backing up left*): Me, frightened? No, no. Not at all. This will be a fine adventure. Besides, I am getting hungry . . . and my wife, Dassie—(*Backs into* CUB, *freezes, turns slowly around, then shrieks*) Ah-h-h! (*Jumps away, screaming*) Look out! A terrifying lion is here. It will eat us up. Hide, everybody! (*Searching about frantically*) Where shall I hide? (*Spies bag*) Inside the bag! (*Climbs in, feet first, and squats, completely hidden.* CUB, *also frightened, exits left, crying.*)

CUB: Mother, help! Meow! Meow! Mother!

KWAMMANGA (*Amused, calling*): Mantis, there is no danger. That was only a lion cub.

MANTIS (*Poking out head*): Really?

KWAMMANGA: Really!

MONGOOSE (*To* MANTIS): You are a coward.

MANTIS: I am not.

MONGOOSE: Then, why did you hide in the bag?

MANTIS: Well, I . . . ah . . . I jumped in here to plan where the meat should go. Now, it is a fine idea for you and Mongoose to go ahead and visit the lions. An even better idea is for me to stay here in the bag and wait. (*Holds bag chin high*) I shall be ready to stack up all the chunks of meat you bring back.

KWAMMANGA (*Sighing*): Oh, all right. Come on, Mongoose. (*Exits left, followed by disgusted* MONGOOSE. MANTIS, *facing audience in dream pose, doesn't see* CUB,

*who sneaks on left and moves stealthily from bush to bush,
now and then peering out at* MANTIS.)

MANTIS: How nice to have such brave, considerate
friends. (CUB *leaps on* MANTIS, *who scrambles from bag,
shrieking.*) Ah-h-h! (*Runs around water hole, screaming;*
CUB *chases him, meowing.*)

ELAND (*Entering left, shouting*): What is going on here?

MANTIS (*Yelling back*): Help me, Wise Eland. The lions
are trying to eat me up.

ELAND (*Shouting*): I see no lions. I only see a little cub. It
cannot hurt you, Mantis.

MANTIS (*Stopping, scratching head*): Hm-m-m! Wise Eland
is right. This creature is a baby, and babies do not
know how to hurt anything. (CUB *grimaces, then tiptoes
over to hide behind a bush.*)

ELAND: Next time, Mantis, before you run away from
nothing, use the brains in that triangular head of
yours.

MANTIS: Yes. Next time I must think. (*Rushes over and
shouts at* CUB) Boo! (CUB *yelps.*) Run to your mother.

CUB (*Exiting left, crying*): Help, Mother! Meow! Meow!
Help!

MANTIS (*Laughing*): There is nothing around here for
me to fear. (*Picks up bag and peers inside*) How silly I
was to be afraid of a baby lion. (*Shouts off left*) Kwammanga! Mongoose! Hurry up! Where are the chunks
of meat?

ELAND (*Crossing right, shaking head*): How is it that sometimes Mantis can be clever and brave. (*To audience*) To
give you an example, he created me, the Eland, from
an old leather sandal. I could go on and on, telling
you stories of the wonderful things Mantis has done.
(*Pantomiming*) Why, once he stole fire from under an
ostrich wing then threw it into the sky. That is how the
sun was born. Another time, he hurled an ostrich

feather into the night and gave us the moon. But, at other times, Mantis is lazy, stupid, and afraid of everything. (*Exits right, shaking head;* MOTHER LION *angrily enters left, unseen by* MANTIS.)

MOTHER LION: Where is the creature who frightened my little baby? (*Sees* MANTIS) Aha! There he is. (*Crosses to* MANTIS, *who doesn't bother to look around, and roars*) How dare you scare a lion cub!

MANTIS (*Still not looking around*): Oh, go away, you insignificant hair ball.

MOTHER LION (*Furiously*): What did you say? (ELAND *reenters, is startled by the scene.*)

MANTIS: You heard me. Rush back to your mother and hide under her belly button.

MOTHER LION (*Roaring*): Gr-r-r! (*Prepares to grab* MANTIS)

MANTIS (*Laughing*): Your pipsqueak roars don't frighten me.

ELAND (*Whispering*): Mantis, Mantis.

MANTIS: Oh, hello, Wise Eland. I took your advice. Before I run, I use the brains in my triangular head.

ELAND (*Whispering*): Yes, but you must also use the big eyes on your funny face.

MANTIS: Use the what?

ELAND (*Yelling*): Use your eyes! Your big eyes! A huge lion crouches behind you.

MANTIS (*Turning to see* LION; *shrieking*): Ah-h-h! (*Leaps away just as* LION *pounces; shouts*) What shall I do? I must use my head *and* my eyes. (*Looks frantically about, sees water hole; suddenly*) Ah ha! I shall plunge into the water hole. (*Leaps into water hole; sound of water splashing*)

LION: Come back here! I hate to swim.

MANTIS (*Sputtering*): I know. I know. Most cats do. That is why I am in the water, and you are on the land.

LION (*Snarling*): All right. I will leave you alone for now. But you'd better stay away from my family.

MANTIS: With pleasure. (LION *gives a final roar, which startles* ELAND *and scares* MANTIS, *then exits left.*)

ELAND (*Calling*): You can come out now, Mantis. Mama lion is gone.

MANTIS (*Crawling out*): Are you sure?

ELAND: Yes.

MANTIS (*Sighing with relief*): That was close. (*Stands and pantomimes shaking off water; looks about fearfully*) I am tired of waiting. When Kwammanga and Mongoose return, tell them they were gone too long. Tell them Mantis decided to go home. (*Crosses to hut, sneaks up to doorway, then peeks inside*) Ah, good. Dassie is taking a nap. (*Stands in dream pose*)

ELAND (*To audience, shrugging*): There are times when each of us is afraid of something. (KWAMMANGA *and* MONGOOSE *reenter, carrying chunks of meat.*)

KWAMMANGA: Where is Mantis? (*During conversation, he packs meat into bag, as does* MONGOOSE.)

ELAND: He went home. He was tired of waiting. (*Exits left*)

MONGOOSE (*Disgusted*): Mantis deserves nothing. He is a lazy, no-good coward. (*Sighs*) Oh, well, I suppose we could give him this small piece of meat. (*Holds it up*)

KWAMMANGA (*Nodding*): When good fortune shows her face, everyone should see it. (*Slings bag over shoulder and crosses up right, exiting;* MONGOOSE *follows, dropping chunk of meat beside dreaming* MANTIS; DASSIE, *appearing in doorway, sees* KWAMMANGA *with the bag and watches* MONGOOSE *leave the meat.*)

DASSIE (*Crossing to* MANTIS): Mantis, my husband.

MANTIS (*Jumping in surprise*): Ah, hello, Dassie, my lovely Rock Rabbit wife.

DASSIE: You are home sooner than I expected. What happened?

MANTIS: Terrible things! We had a dreadful fight with the lions. They ate Kwammanga and Mongoose. Only by using the brains in my triangular head, the big eyes on my funny face, and the long legs beneath my body was I able to escape. Therefore, I could not bring back any meat.

DASSIE: What is that beside you?

MANTIS: Beside me? (*Astonished to see meat*) Hm-m-m, well . . . ah . . I found that piece of meat. It must be the one I saw in my dream.

DASSIE: You don't say.

MANTIS: I do say.

DASSIE (*Shaking finger*): For shame, Mantis. You are lying.

MANTIS: Lying? Me?

DASSIE: The lions did not eat Kwammanga and Mongoose. A few moments ago I saw Kwammanga with a large, full sack. I also saw Mongoose. It was he who dropped that meat beside you. And the whole time you stood there, staring at the sky, dreaming.

MANTIS (*Wincing*): How dreadful! (*Stiffens, arms to side*) Alas, my dream has gone. (*Swallows hard, then nods*) Yes, Dassie, I must admit I have been lazy and afraid. What is worse, I have lied to you. Now you are angry with me, and you have every reason to be so. (*Hangs head*) Forgive me, dear wife. Here, take all this meat. (*Hands over meat*) I shall go into our house and bury my foolish head in a corner. (*Exits into hut;* DASSIE *examines meat;* ELAND *reenters, crossing to her.*)

ELAND: Dassie, I see that you have received a gift from the lions. It will make a delicious supper. (*Slyly*) Did Mantis bring the meat home?

DASSIE (*Smiling*): In a roundabout way, yes.

ELAND: Where is Mantis?

DASSIE: In the house, dreaming new dreams. And now, excuse me, Wise Eland. I want to cook this meat for supper. (*Smiles*) Mantis and I will share it. (*Exits into hut*)

ELAND (*To audience*): There is some of Mantis in each of us. Nobody can be perfect. Sometimes we are lazy; other times we work hard. Today we may be cowards; tomorrow we could be brave. To tell a lie is a childish thing to do, but who among us has not told one? To own up to our faults and apologize is the beginning of wisdom. Most important, learn a lesson from Dassie, the Rock Rabbit wife: Those who understand and forgive the imperfections of others are the wisest of all. (*Curtain*)

THE END

TWO FROM ABUNUWAS

TWO FROM ABUNUWAS

Where Arabic culture has strongly influenced the lives of African people, especially along the coast of East Africa, in North Africa, and on a number of offshore islands such as Madagascar and Zanzibar, many tales are told of a trickster-hero called Abunuwas, also known as Kibunwasi.

In the 8th century A.D. there lived a man by the name of Abu Nuwas, a Persian poet who resided in Baghdad and was a favorite of the Caliph. When stories about him are told in Africa, they often gather attributes of the particular locality of the storyteller. Whereas in the Middle East Abunuwas had a friend who was a millet farmer, in Algiers the friend might be a rug merchant, and instead of going to the market place, he might go to a casbah. Whatever the habitat, Abunuwas remains a simple but clever man who either outwits those who attempt to fool him or helps solve a problem that stumps a friend.

Two from Abunuwas

Tales from North Africa

I. THE STOLEN SHOES

Characters

STORYTELLER
ABUNUWAS
DONKEY
HAJI, *rug merchant*
INA, *his wife*
ALI, *shoe merchant*
LEWA, *his wife*

BEFORE RISE: STORYTELLER, *carrying small, rolled-up oriental rug, enters left before curtain, crosses to extreme right, spreads rug, and then sits on it, facing audience, remaining there during play.*

STORYTELLER (*Smiling and bowing head*): I am an old storyteller. I travel with my son, his family, and a group of friends across the harsh Sahara Desert. We ride our camels from one village to another, and in the evening, while my son sells cloth to the villagers, I weave stories for the children.

"Tell us a funny tale," they cry. "Tell about the clever man, the one who lived long ago and far away."

119

"You mean Abunuwas?" They all nod and laugh. "Indeed, I shall," say I. "Listen carefully. Here is the tale of the stolen shoes."

* * * * *

SETTING: *Backdrop painting of sand dunes and part of a North African village. Date palm trees are right and left. Under left palm is large, flat rock used as seat.*
AT RISE: ABUNUWAS *sits cross-legged on rock, composing a poem. He stares ahead, hands under bearded chin, thinking.* DONKEY *stands left, braying unhappily.*

ABUNUWAS (*Waving to hush* DONKEY): Yes, yes, my hungry donkey, I shall feed you soon. Now, though, I am creating food for the mind. (DONKEY *gives disgusted snort.* ABUNUWAS *raises arms, excitedly*). Thank you, friend donkey. That is a splendid idea for a poem. (*Silently recites poem, lips moving rapidly, hands waving dramatically.* HAJI *hurriedly enters right, barefoot. He stops a moment in amusement to watch* ABUNUWAS, *then hurries to him and clears throat to gain attention.* ABUNUWAS *bows head.*) Salaam, Haji. I trust you sell more rugs than rats chew up.
HAJI (*Bowing*): Salaam, Abunuwas. In the casbah, I sell my merchandise so quickly, no rats have an opportunity. And you? Are poems (*Pantomiming*) pouring from your head as sand slips through a man's fingers?
ABUNUWAS (*With mock alarm*): I hope not. (*Pantomiming*) I would not wish my words to be as dry as sand nor as lost as what slips from a man's hand.
HAJI (*Smiling*): As always, you are clever. That, Abunuwas, is why I am here.
ABUNUWAS: Do you have a problem?
HAJI: Yes.
ABUNUWAS (*Looking at* HAJI's *feet*): It must be important,

or you would not run here without first putting on shoes.

HAJI: My shoes *are* the problem. They have just been stolen.

ABUNUWAS: Stolen, you say. Too bad, Haji. Tell me more.

HAJI: This afternoon, I visited the house of Ali, the shoe merchant. My wife, Ina, came with me, claiming it was better than being left home alone.

ABUNUWAS: Poor Ina. (*Shaking finger in reproach*) You are out visiting friends every afternoon and evening.

HAJI (*Spreading arms*): I like companionship. (*Smiling*) Besides, it saves money to drink another man's tea or eat his food.

ABUNUWAS: I see. And so, this afternoon you went to the home of the shoe merchant to drink a hot glass of tea?

HAJI (*Nodding and pantomiming*): Today at my shop in the casbah, I beat the dust out of an exceptionally dirty rug. That task, along with the growing heat of the morning, parched my throat beyond belief. I stopped at home to wash my hands and face. My wife begged to accompany me to Ali's house, so I let her come along. As is the custom, we left our shoes outside the door. Then Lewa, Ali's wife, led us inside. An hour later, when we came outside, my wife's shoes were there, but mine were gone.

ABUNUWAS: Do you suspect anyone?

HAJI: It could have been Ali. He left the room once, and I owe him money for the shoes. It could have been his wife or my wife. They were in another part of the house while Ali and I drank tea. My wife could have done it as a joke; Lewa could have done it if she thinks I visit too often. (*Shrugs*) They all said they knew nothing about my shoes. Maybe a thief on the street stole them.

ABUNUWAS (*Stroking beard thoughtfully*): You can rule out a street thief, Haji. There are many clean shoes beside doorways. A street thief would not take shoes dusty from beating a rug. (HAJI *shrugs and throws up arms in bewilderment.*)

HAJI: Alas, I was planning to visit another friend for dinner tonight. How can I go without shoes? (ABUNUWAS *suddenly gets idea and claps hands.*)

ABUNUWAS: Ah, ho! Haji, tell Ali, Lewa, and your wife, Ina, to come to my rock in half an hour.

HAJI: Why?

ABUNUWAS: Your shoes will then be found. (*Chuckles*) All will come, Haji, for they will be curious.

HAJI: So be it, Abunuwas. In half an hour. (*Runs off right.* ABUNUWAS *climbs down from rock.*)

ABUNUWAS: Now, I have time to pick fragrant mint for my supper tonight. (*Crossing to scratch* DONKEY's *ears*) And then, my long-eared friend, I shall feed you, and we will have a little conversation in private. (DONKEY *brays happily.* ABUNUWAS *starts to exit left. Blackout of a few seconds. When lights come up,* ABUNUWAS *is sitting on rock as before.* DONKEY *stands behind rock so tail is hidden from audience.* HAJI, INA, ALI, *and* LEWA *enter right.* INA *has* HAJI's *shoes hidden in her sleeves, one on each side. They cross to rock. All bow.*) Salaam, my friends.

OTHERS: Salaam, Abunuwas.

HAJI: Have you found my shoes?

ABUNUWAS: Not I.

HAJI (*Disappointed*): No?

ABUNUWAS: No. But my donkey knows who took them. He knows everything.

OTHERS (*In surprise*): Everything?

ABUNUWAS (*Nodding*): He will name the thief.

HAJI: I have never heard of a talking donkey.

ABUNUWAS: Some creatures are smarter than others. My donkey is exceptionally smart.

HAJI: Then why does he hide behind your rock?

ABUNUWAS: He does not hide; he waits. Before he can name the thief, he wishes to perform a test.

OTHERS (*To each other, ad lib*): A test? What kind of test? (*Etc.*)

ABUNUWAS (*Jumping off rock*): My donkey wishes to see us separately. He asks each (*Pantomiming*) to pull his tail once with the right hand. When the thief pulls his tail, my donkey will bray loudly. Then we will know who the thief is.

LEWA: You mean, only by pulling the donkey's tail will the thief be known?

ABUNUWAS: Yes. I shall go first so you may be sure I did not steal Haji's shoes. (*Crosses behind rock. Others put hands to ears to listen. This is repeated each time person crosses behind rock.* ABUNUWAS *quickly returns.*) There. I pulled the tail and nothing happened. You are next, Haji.

HAJI: Why me? My shoes were the ones stolen.

ALI: Ha! You probably hid them. You do not wish to pay me for them.

HAJI: What? Ridiculous! I will show you I am not the thief. (*Crosses behind rock, quickly returning*) There. I pulled the donkey's tail and nothing happened. You go, Ali. Perhaps you stole my shoes. You want to sell them again.

ALI: What? Ridiculous! I will show you I am not the thief. (*Crosses behind rock, quickly returning*) There. I pulled the donkey's tail and nothing happened. I think your wife, Ina, stole the shoes. A barefoot husband cannot wander far from home.

INA: What? Ridiculous! I will show you I am not the

thief. (*Crosses behind rock, quickly returning*) There. I pulled the donkey's tail and nothing happened. It must be you, Lewa. You never have approved of Haji drinking so much of your husband's tea or suddenly showing up in the evening for dinner.

LEWA: What? Ridiculous! I will show you I am not the thief. (*Crosses behind rock, returning quickly*) There. I pulled the donkey's tail and nothing happened. (*All shrug and look at each other suspiciously.* DONKEY *crosses down left, braying loudly and angrily, looking back at tail and then sitting on it. This startles everyone.*)

HAJI: Abunuwas, *now* your donkey brays. What is he saying? (ABUNUWAS *crosses to* DONKEY, *whispers in each ear, listens at* DONKEY'S *mouth, nods solemnly, and then returns to sit on rock.*)

ABUNUWAS: My donkey tells me there is more to the test.

OTHERS (*To each other*): More to the test?

ABUNUWAS: Each of us must touch the top of my nose with a finger of the right hand. It is a secret sign. (*Touches nose with index finger of right hand*) See. I will be first. Now, you Haji, and then the others. (*Each in turn passes by and touches* ABUNUWAS's *nose with index finger of right hand. After all have done so,* ABUNUWAS *stands on rock.*) Ah, ha! I know the thief.

OTHERS: You do? Who is it? (*Etc.* ABUNUWAS *raises index finger heavenward, looking at each person, then suddenly points to* INA.)

ABUNUWAS: Ina is the one. (*Leaps from rock*) Haji, your wife took your shoes. I am certain of it. (DONKEY *brays loudly.*)

OTHERS (*Pointing at her*): Ina? (*A moment of silence as others stare at her.* INA *at first shakes head, then breaks down.*)

INA (*Tearfully*): Oh, all right! I am the one. I hid Haji's shoes. (*Lets shoes fall from sleeves. Others gasp.* HAJI *glowers and puts on shoes.* INA *speaks in rush of words.*)

Oh, Haji, I only wanted to teach you a lesson. Every day after work you run to visit someone for tea. Every night you run off again. You never want to stay home with me. I hid your shoes, hoping you would stay home with me this evening. (*Bursts into tears*)

HAJI: There, there. Stop crying, Ina. You sound like an overloaded camel.

INA (*Sniffing*): Forgive me, husband. I am deeply sorry. But, it is only because I care for you so much that I desire your company. (*Wails.* LEWA *runs to comfort her.*)

HAJI: Be still, wife. I must think about this. (*Scratches head and then gets idea. Smiles and spreads arms*) Ali, would you and your wife care to join us for dinner this evening, in *my* (*Pointing to self*) home? I might even pay you for the shoes.

ALI (*Rubbing hands*): Certainly! It will be a happy occasion.

HAJI: Good. (*Pats* INA's *shoulders and speaks softly so others do not hear*) I realize I have neglected you for too long, my dear. (INA *smiles.* HAJI *moves hastily away and gestures to* ABUNUWAS.) Excuse me, Abunuwas, would you also like to come to dinner?

ABUNUWAS: No, thank you, Haji. I have a poem to finish.

HAJI: Another time, perhaps. I am most grateful for your help. May all your poems be as clever as your donkey. (ABUNUWAS *strikes forehead in mock alarm as others bow and then exit right.*)

ABUNUWAS (*Sighing*): People are strange. Everyone wants the answer to a problem. Few care how a problem is solved. (DONKEY *brays and crosses to get* ABUNUWAS *to scratch his ears.*) Ah, my donkey, at least *you* want to know how I solved the problem. (*Climbs on rock, sitting as before, speaking to* DONKEY) You remember I rubbed mint on your tail this afternoon?

You see, I knew the guilty person would *not* pull your tail for fear you would bray. So (*Points right finger in air*) the person whose right hand did not smell of mint (*Places finger on nose*) was obviously the thief. (DONKEY *brays with laughter.* ABUNUWAS *joins in laughter.*) Yes, yes, my friend. It is another splendid idea for a poem. (*Curtain starts to close while* ABUNUWAS *silently composes, arms waving, lips moving, as at start of play. Curtain*)

*   *   *   *   *

II. THE BORROWED COOKING POT

Characters

STORYTELLER
ABUNUWAS
HAJI, *rug merchant*
INA, *his wife*
DONKEY

BEFORE RISE: STORYTELLER *sits on rug, as before.*

STORYTELLER: My favorite Abunuwas story is about the borrowed cooking pot. This tale is told in different ways in different places—all across Northern Africa, through Arabia, Iran, and Iraq. Here is the way I tell the tale. (*Curtain opens.*)

*   *   *   *   *

SETTING: *Same.*

AT RISE: ABUNUWAS *rushes on left.*

ABUNUWAS (*Calling*): Haji. Haji.

HAJI (*Entering right*): Yes, Abunuwas?

ABUNUWAS *and* HAJI (*Bowing to each other*): Salaam, my friend.

ABUNUWAS: Exalted rug merchant, I have a favor to ask.

HAJI: What is it, great poet?

ABUNUWAS: May I borrow a large cooking pot for making couscous?*

HAJI: Hm-m-m, well, I am not in the habit of lending my valuables, but for you . . . (*Calling right*) Ina, my wife, come here.

INA (*Entering*): Yes, husband. (HAJI *crosses to her.*)

HAJI: Abunuwas wants to borrow a large cooking pot for couscous.

INA: Since he has always helped us, we should certainly help him. (*Turns to exit right*)

HAJI: Wait, wait! (*With sidelong glances at* ABUNUWAS, *speaking so* ABUNUWAS *cannot hear*) Do not bring our good cooking pot, Ina. Bring the one with the hole in it.

INA: But, Haji—

HAJI (*Interrupting*): Sh-h-h, do as I say. I would not lend our best cooking pot even to the King of Morocco.

INA: But, how can he cook in a leaky pot?

HAJI (*Shrewdly*): He will have it repaired, of course. Then we will have *two* fine pots. Now, hurry and bring the old one here. (INA *shrugs, then exits right.* HAJI *crosses to* ABUNUWAS, *smiling.*) Ina will return in a moment with the cooking pot.

ABUNUWAS: I am grateful for your kindness. (INA *returns with large, old pot and gives it to* HAJI, *who inspects pot, with back to* ABUNUWAS, *nods, and then dramatically presents it to* ABUNUWAS.)

HAJI (*Bowing*): May your couscous be as good as your poems.

---

*Couscous, a North African dish, is made from steamed semolina, a milled product of a kind of wheat, with various types of stew poured over it.

ABUNUWAS (*Bowing*): Thank you, Haji. May your day be as good as your cooking pot. (HAJI *looks startled, then quickly smiles and exits right. Meanwhile,* ABUNUWAS *holds pot up to light and notes hole in bottom.*) Well, well, my friend Haji gives me a pot with a hole in the bottom. (*Chuckles*) He probably thinks I will repair it. (*Exits left, still chuckling. Blackout. As lights go up a few seconds later,* ABUNUWAS *reenters, carrying the large pot with a small pot inside. Calling*) Haji. Haji. (HAJI *reenters.*) A wonderful thing has happened.

HAJI: A wonderful thing?

ABUNUWAS: Yes, it's about this leaky pot of yours.

HAJI (*Faking surprise*): Leaky? Do you mean there was a hole in it? Oh, I am so sorry. Thank you for repairing it.

ABUNUWAS: I did not repair it. But look at what is inside.

HAJI (*Looking*): A small cooking pot.

ABUNUWAS: Yes. A miracle has happened. Just as I was about to use your cooking pot, it suddenly gave birth to a cooking pot just like it, only half as big.

HAJI: That is difficult to believe. (*Holds up small pot*)

ABUNUWAS: I know. Lately miracles keep happening in my house. Why, only yesterday, another friend lent me a large, beautiful teapot, and it gave birth to a small, beautiful teapot.

HAJI: Hm-m-m. Amazing. (*Suddenly yells*) Ina, Ina, come quickly. (INA *enters.* HAJI *crosses quickly to her.*) Look, we have another pot for our home. (INA *holds small pot up to light.*)

INA: It has a hole in it. It is no good. (HAJI *speaks so* ABUNUWAS *won't hear.*)

HAJI: Sh-h-h. I think Abunuwas has gone crazy.

INA (*Loudly*): What?

HAJI: Sh-h-h, sh-h-h! He believes miracles are happening at his house. (*Taps head, indicating* ABUNUWAS *is unbalanced*) Obviously, he placed this little pot in here. However, he claims our big, leaky pot gave birth to a small, leaky pot. Furthermore, he claims that yesterday a big, beautiful teapot gave birth to a small, beautiful teapot. (*Chuckles*) Therefore, if we lend him our brand new pot, surely it will give birth to a pot just as new. Thus, we will obtain two fine pots for our home. (*Rubs hands greedily. Loudly*) Ina, bring our large, new cooking pot for the great poet.

INA (*Rolling eyes*): As you wish, husband. (*Exits right, carrying old pots and muttering*) This business sounds silly to me.

HAJI (*To* ABUNUWAS): Nothing is too good for you, my friend. (INA *reenters with large, new pot.* HAJI *presents it to* ABUNUWAS *with bow. Dramatically*) I pray for more miracles in your home.

ABUNUWAS (*Bowing*): How very thoughtful of you. (*Exits left.* HAJI *exits right, rubbing hands in expectation. Blackout. When lights go up a few seconds later,* ABUNUWAS *is sitting cross-legged on rock.* DONKEY *is left.* HAJI *reenters right.*)

HAJI *and* ABUNUWAS (*Bowing to each other*): Salaam, my friend.

HAJI: How was your couscous?

ABUNUWAS: Delicious.

HAJI: Good, good. (*Rubbing hands together*) And did you have another miracle at your house?

ABUNUWAS (*With mock sadness*): I have news for you, Haji.

HAJI: About my cooking pot? Did it give birth?

ABUNUWAS (*Shaking head*): No.

HAJI (*Annoyed*): Then bring it back to me at once.

ABUNUWAS: I wish I could, but unfortunately your cooking pot died.

HAJI: Died!

ABUNUWAS (*Gazing upward*): May it rest in a world of peace.

HAJI (*Crossing angrily to rock*): Abunuwas! You know very well a cooking pot cannot die.

ABUNUWAS: It cannot? But Haji, you were quick to believe your leaky old pot could give birth. You prayed your fine, new pot would also give birth. (*Rising with outstretched arms*) And any fool knows where there is life there is also death. (*Folding arms*) So, you must believe that your cooking pot died. It was very sudden, you know. I buried it just this morning. (HAJI *strikes head in alarm.*)

HAJI: Buried it! Where?

ABUNUWAS: In the river, where all good pots go at the end of their days on earth. Please give my sympathy to your wife. (HAJI *staggers backward.*)

HAJI: Buried in the river! Oh, no! My best cooking pot is gone. (*Moves right, mumbling, tearing at robe, acting a bit crazy*) I am a fool. I have killed my best pot. (*Exits right as* DONKEY *brays with laughter.* ABUNUWAS *holds up arm to stop braying.*)

ABUNUWAS: We must not laugh at this serious time. (DONKEY *snorts with disgust.*) Ah, thank you, friend donkey. That is another fine idea for a poem. (*Curtain slowly closes while* ABUNUWAS *silently ad libs poem, as at start of play.* STORYTELLER *rises, bows to audience, then rolls up rug and exits.*)

THE END

WHO WEARS THE NECKLACE NOW?

WHO WEARS THE NECKLACE NOW?

On the grasslands of Kenya, and extending down into Tanzania, live a proud people known as the Masai (or Maasai). A nomadic people, their movements are dictated by the need to find grazing areas and water for herds of cattle, their most treasured possessions. Traditionally, great importance is placed on ceremonials, especially those relating to becoming a warrior. A tall, thin people, the Masai appear most impressive in their colorful dress. The women create beautiful beadwork and decorate themselves heavily with necklaces, earrings, and bracelets; the men also wear earrings, but their necklaces are simple strands.

As civilization and land restrictions press in around the Masai, their ceremonials and traditional ways are disappearing. Today, many Masai have settled in villages or left their tribe, going away to live in the city of Nairobi.

Who Wears the Necklace Now?

A Kenyan folktale

Characters

STORYTELLER
WARRIOR MEMUSI
HARE
CHORUS (*2 or more*)
ANTELOPE
FIRE
WATERHOLE
ELEPHANT
ACACIA TREE
TERMITE HILL
TWO HYENAS

SETTING: *Southern Kenya. Backdrop has painting of grassy plains with Mt. Kilimanjaro in the distance and a Masai village to the left, painted as if continuing offstage. Up right is a short, vine-like rope, appearing to be growing along the ground.*

AT RISE: WARRIOR MEMUSI, *wearing necklace and with pouch slung across one shoulder, stands left, on one leg in Masai fashion, leaning on his spear. He warms himself by* FIRE, *who sits crouched.* ACACIA TREE *stands up right, next to rope, with arms outstretched.* TERMITE HILL *is nearby.* WATERHOLE *lies center, hidden under blanket.* STORY-TELLER, *carrying rattle, and* CHORUS *enter and sit to one*

133

side of stage, STORYTELLER *in center of group. Except for first and last lines of play,* STORYTELLER *and* CHORUS *chant their lines to rhythm of rattle.*

STORYTELLER: Once upon a time, when Hare hopped to the waterhole for her usual morning drink, she met the Masai warrior named Memusi. (HARE *hops in right, carrying spearhead, and pantomimes drinking at* WATER- HOLE.)

WARRIOR (*Calling*): Good morning, Hare.

HARE: Hello, Memusi. Warming yourself by the fire this cool morning?

WARRIOR: Yes, but the hot sun will soon begin.

HARE: True. (*Crossing to him*) I was planning to visit your village today. I found this spearhead in the bush and thought it might be useful to someone. (*Hands it to* WARRIOR)

WARRIOR: An excellent spearhead. It would be a good replacement for this old one. (*Indicates his spearhead*)

HARE: What will you give me for it?

WARRIOR (*Thinking*): How about my necklace? (*Handing it to* HARE) It is a particularly fine one.

HARE: Indeed, it is. (*Nods*) Agreed. A good trade for us both. (*During following chant,* WARRIOR *puts spearhead in pouch, and* HARE *puts on necklace and hops over to admire her reflection in* WATERHOLE.)

STORYTELLER: How beautiful is the necklace,

CHORUS: Made of tiny, shiny beads,
   Rows and rows of brilliant beads—

ALL: The necklace worn by Hare. (ANTELOPE *enters right, prancing affectedly.*)

HARE: Antelope, I have a new necklace. Doesn't it look marvelous on me?

ANTELOPE (*Snippily*): Oh, it's all right, but I have seen prettier beads. Let me try it. (*During chant,* HARE *gives necklace to* ANTELOPE, *who wears it, admiring her reflection in* WATERHOLE.)

STORYTELLER: How beautiful is the necklace,
CHORUS: Made of tiny, shiny beads,
   Rows and rows of brilliant beads—
ALL: The necklace worn by Antelope.
ANTELOPE: Hare, I have decided I like this necklace
   after all. I shall keep it for myself.
HARE: What? You can't do that. It is mine. Give it back.
   (*Holds out paw*)
ANTELOPE: You will have to catch me first. And you
   know how fast an Antelope can run. (*Exits right, run-
   ning and laughing*)
HARE (*Sputtering*): Well, of all the—I can't believe that!
   This is awful. (*Calling*) Memusi, Antelope stole my
   necklace. (*Pleading*) Please, run out there and hurl
   your spear at her.
WARRIOR: Why?
HARE (*Indignantly*): Because *you* have my spearhead, and
   Antelope stole my necklace.
WARRIOR: Just a minute, Hare. In the first place, I am a
   warrior, not a hunter. In the second place, Antelope
   has not hurt me. Sorry, Hare. This is your bad luck,
   not mine. (*Exits left. During chant* HARE *hops around,
   shaking her paws in agitation. After each chant she grows
   louder and angrier.*)
STORYTELLER: Warrior won't shoot Antelope,
CHORUS: Who wears the necklace now.
HARE (*Crossing to* FIRE): Fire, please listen to me. (FIRE
   hisses and spits when speaking.)
FIRE (*Rising*): What is your problem?
HARE: In order to get my stolen necklace back, I need
   Memusi to spear Antelope, but he won't do it.
FIRE: A shame. What is it I can do?
HARE: Burn up Memusi's spear.
FIRE: Why?
HARE: Because it isn't fair for Memusi to have a spear
   when I don't have my necklace.

FIRE: Life isn't necessarily fair, you know. And, since Memusi has always shown me respect, I will not burn his spear. (*During chant* FIRE *settles down and* HARE *stomps about, shaking her paws in the direction of the village and* FIRE.)

STORYTELLER: Fire won't burn Warrior's spear,

CHORUS: Warrior won't shoot Antelope,

ALL: Who wears the necklace now.

HARE (*Louder*): Waterhole, listen to me.

WATERHOLE (*Rising majestically; speaking with English accent*): What on earth is wrong, Hare?

HARE (*Pointing*): Fire won't help me.

WATERHOLE: I say, what rotten luck!

HARE: So put out the fire with your water.

WATERHOLE (*Astonished*): Not a very sporting thing to do, old chap. You jolly well better calm down before you go up in a puff of smoke. Now, excuse me. It is time for the elephants to visit. (*Sinks back down and disappears under blanket during chant, while* HARE *fumes about. As chant progresses,* STORYTELLER *and* CHORUS *encourage audience also to chant, continuing this throughout play.*)

STORYTELLER: Waterhole won't douse the Fire,

CHORUS: Fire won't burn Warrior's spear,

Warrior won't shoot Antelope,

ALL: Who wears the necklace now. (ELEPHANT *lumbers in, trumpeting, and crosses to* WATERHOLE.)

HARE (*Yelling*): Elephant, drink up all the water.

ELEPHANT: Why?

HARE: Because I am mad at Waterhole.

ELEPHANT: Hm-m-m! Anger is clouding your reason. I refuse to drink all the water. Have you forgotten the law of the bush—*only drink what is necessary?* Shame on you! (*During chant,* ELEPHANT *pantomimes drinking from* WATERHOLE *and then crosses to rest under* ACACIA TREE, *while* HARE *leaps about with increasing fury.*)

STORYTELLER: Elephant won't overdrink,
CHORUS: Waterhole won't douse the Fire,
   Fire won't burn Warrior's spear,
   Warrior won't shoot Antelope,
ALL: Who wears the necklace now.
HARE (*Shrieking*): Termite Hill!
TERMITE HILL: Yes, Hare?
HARE: Eat Acacia Tree.
TERMITE HILL: We've been eating wood all day. My termites are full. Go away and leave us alone.
HARE (*Screaming*): Ah-h-h-h! (*During chant she completely loses control, falling to ground, pounding it, rolling about, shaking paws in air, etc. Chant goes faster and faster, as does* HARE. ELEPHANT *exits right in disgust.*)
STORYTELLER: Hill won't gobble Acacia Tree,
CHORUS: Tree won't fall on Elephant.
   Elephant won't overdrink,
   Waterhole won't douse the Fire,
   Fire won't burn Warrior's spear,
   Warrior won't shoot Antelope,
ALL: Who wears the necklace now. (HYENAS *enter left, loping and yipping.* HARE, *seeing them, jumps up excitedly.*)
HARE: Hooray, Hyenas! (HYENAS *stop, perplexed, sniffing in* HARE's *direction.*) At last, I have found creatures who won't bother to ask me *why.* Hyenas don't care if anything is right or wrong. (*Rushing to them*) Hyenas, I can direct you to delicious Antelope, who is certainly near here. (HYENAS *look interested.*) Now, what do you say about that?
1ST HYENA: I say foolishness kills the one who owns it.
2ND HYENA: And Hare, you are quite foolish.
HYENAS (*In unison*): We think *you* would make a delightful breakfast. (*Laughing, they pounce on* HARE, *who shrieks and squirms.*)
HARE (*Screaming*): Help, help! Hyenas are going to eat

me. (TREE, FIRE, HILL, *and* WATERHOLE *look at* HARE *in unison, then put hands over eyes and turn away.* WARRIOR *and* ELEPHANT *peer on stage and do the same.*) Wait a minute, wait a minute, you can't eat me now.

HYENAS (*In unison*): Of course we can.

HARE: No, you can't. I'm not—I'm not—(*Suddenly; smiling at audience*) I am not wearing my magic necklace.

1ST HYENA (*Looking at audience*): That's a new one.

HARE: Yes, yes, the great magic necklace. If I don't wear it, my meat will be poison, and if you eat me, you will certainly *die.*

2ND HYENA: I have never heard of a Hare wearing a necklace in order to be good food.

HARE: As a matter of fact, this development just happened today.

1ST HYENA: Well, where is this magic necklace?

HARE: Antelope is wearing it. She's out there in the bush. (*Pointing right*)

2ND HYENA: Let's tie up Hare so she won't get away.

1ST HYENA: Good idea! (*Sits on* HARE'S *stomach as* 2ND HYENA *sees rope by* TREE *and pantomimes pulling it from ground*) Then we can hunt for Antelope, get the necklace, and have two delicious meals. (2ND HYENA *returns with rope and during chant they tie* HARE'S *paws together so they stick in air. Chant increases in speed as it progresses.*)

STORYTELLER: Hyenas eat most anything, but

CHORUS: Hill won't gobble Acacia Tree,
    Tree won't fall on Elephant
    Elephant won't overdrink,
    Waterhole won't douse the Fire,
    Fire won't burn Warrior's spear
    Warrior won't shoot Antelope,

ALL: Who wears the necklace now. (HYENAS *exit right.*)

HARE (*Wailing*): Oh-h-h, what a terrible thing I have brought upon myself. (*To audience*) I must think of something clever to get out of this mess. (ANTELOPE *reenters, prancing, sees* HARE *and giggles.*)

ANTELOPE: My goodness, Hare, why are you all tied up?

HARE: Antelope, you are in great danger.

ANTELOPE: From what?

HARE: Hyenas are hunting for you. (ANTELOPE *gasps and looks furtively around.*) They are determined to catch you.

ANTELOPE: Dear me, why?

HARE: Because you are wearing the magic necklace that makes you good to eat. (ANTELOPE *touches necklace in horror.*)

ANTELOPE: This necklace makes me good to eat?

HARE: Yes. I am glad you are wearing it while I am safe here.

ANTELOPE: If you are so safe, why are you tied up?

HARE (*Hesitating*): Well, I am in a special safe position. I couldn't hold all four paws up this way without the aid of vines. So, some passing friends tied them up for me.

ANTELOPE (*Warily*): What makes you think your position is so safe?

HARE: It has to be. When the Hyenas saw I wasn't wearing the magic necklace and was locked into the safe position, they took off after you.

ANTELOPE: I gather it was you who told them I wore the necklace.

HARE (*Sheepishly*): I'm sorry, Antelope. Forgive me.

ANTELOPE (*Furiously*): No, I won't. To show you how angry I am, I shall untie you from your safe position and make you wear this magic necklace. (*Puts necklace on* HARE)

HARE (*In mock fear*): Oh, no, no, Antelope, have pity on me.

ANTELOPE: Out here in the bush, it is every creature for

itself. (*Quickly unties* HARE, *who jumps up.* HYENAS *yip off right.* HARE *and* ANTELOPE *see them coming.*)

HARE: Here come the Hyenas. Antelope, quickly, get into the safe position. I must hop for my life. (*During chant,* HARE *exits left at fast hop, while* ANTELOPE *lies on back with hooves in air.* HYENAS *reenter and curiously circle* ANTELOPE *as* CHORUS *rises, leading audience in faster and faster chant.*)

CHORUS: Hyenas eat most anything, but . . .
> Hill won't gobble Acacia Tree,
> Tree won't fall on Elephant.
> Elephant won't overdrink,
> Waterhole won't douse the Fire,
> Fire won't burn Warrior's spear,
> Warrior won't shoot Antelope,

ALL: And (*Shouting*) Hare wears the necklace now. (HYENAS *pounce on* ANTELOPE, *who squeals in terror as curtain quickly closes.*)

STORYTELLER (*Rising*): That, my friends, is the end of gullible Antelope—and, also, of my story.

THE END

Production Notes

ANANSI, THE AFRICAN SPIDER

Characters: 11 male or female.

Playing Time: 20 minutes.

Costumes: Animals wear heads made of papier-mâché or paper bag masks. Anansi has two sets of false legs strapped to his body, giving appearance of eight legs in all. Storytellers, Nyame, Forest King, and Tall-Tale Man wear tribal head masks made of papier-mâché. Nyame's mask represents the sun; Forest King wears crown and carries a staff.

Properties: Three African rattles; large "talking" drum.

Setting: Equatorial Africa (Ghana). There is a painted backdrop showing equatorial forest; backdrop curtain may also be used, with vines and shrubbery set in front of it. For Scene 1, cardboard cut-outs of ḳola nut tree and berry bush are near center. Hornets' nest hangs from bush, and calabash gourd lies on ground. There is a tall stool up center. Paper and cotton clouds are attached to stool, indicating sky.

Lighting: No special effects. Blue flood may be used in night scene of "The First Talking Drum."

Sound: Crocodile chomping on rock and losing teeth; hornets buzzing; drumbeats; chomping, chewing, pounding, etc., as giant drum is built. (Crew of three can make sound effects offstage.)

IJAPA, THE TORTOISE

Characters: 4 male; 2 female; 6 male or female for Priest, Attendant, and Spirits; as many extras as desired for Villagers.

Playing Time: 20 minutes.

Costumes: Nigerian dress. Bush Spirits and Shango Priest wear tribal masks made of papier-mâché. Priest has anklets made of shells strung together and wears raffia costume. Oba wears fringed crown and bib made of cardboard covered with glue and sprinkled with tiny beads in a design. Ijapa and Yanrinbo wear large papier-mâché turtle shells attached to their backs by belts, or, they may wear Nigerian costumes and pantomime the turtle-shell business indicated in text.

Properties: Palm tree (hollow trunk of papier-mâché, with holes for eyes, painted brown, with brown cloth roots to conceal Ijapa when he wears tree, and branches of straightened coat-hanger wire covered with fringed green paper), three yams, nuts, utensils, cloth, and other market-place items (real or pantomimed), gourd rattle, staff (if possible, find a picture of a carved Nigerian "oshe shango" staff and make a copy of it in papier-mâché), large and small bells with striker stick, vine-like rope, water jar, toy or cardboard machete, shoulder bag pouch containing kernels of corn (real or pantomimed), fringed umbrella, palm frond.

Setting: Scene 1, a Nigerian village, and Scene 2, the Nigerian bush. For both scenes, there is a dark backdrop curtain, with cardboard cut-outs of bushes, trees, and huts attached (or free standing). There is a clump of bushes up left in Scene 1, which is moved to up

center for Scene 2. There is a throne-stool at center for Scene 1, with the hollow palm tree (see *Properties*) at right. They are removed for Scene 2.
Lighting: Blackouts, as indicated in text.
Sound: Live or recorded African music, as indicated in text.

TWO DILEMMA TALES

Characters: 5 male; 3 female; 2 male or female for Spirits; as many male or female as desired for Villagers; extras if desired for Spirits.
Playing Time: 20 minutes.
Costumes: West African. Chief wears headdress and carries a staff. Spirits wear weird papier-mâché masks with raffia attached to bottom of masks and extending to floor, hiding body.
Properties: Tall African drum, two cloth bundles, pouch, honey pot with shoulder strap (small waste basket or large can), spears for Chief and Villagers of wood or rubber (may be pantomimed), wooden stool.
Setting: A West African village. Backdrop shows rain forest with village huts. In first scene, part of a hut with doorway is at left, angled so rest of hut seems to be offstage. In second scene, hut is moved to center. Hut may be made from a very large cardboard box. To make circular pointed roof for hut, put a tall pole anchored in a can of sand inside box and projecting through top of box. String wires from top of pole to top edge of box, and lay raffia or palm branches over wire structure.
Lighting: Lights dim and brighten, Scene 1, as indicated in text.
Sound: Jungle animal sounds, as indicated in text.

AFRICAN TRIO

Characters: 6 male; 5 female; 9 male or female, including Storytellers. Property Girl is a non-speaking part.
Playing Time: 20 minutes.
Costumes: The Storytellers and human characters wear the costumes of the tribe of their story. The Princess must have sandals, a headdress, cloak, and jewels, worn over a simple dress. The animals can wear large paper bag or papier-mâché masks.
Properties: African drum, mbira or other African harp, yellow pot, red pot, yellow and red cardboard discs, blue crepe paper streamers, cut-outs of palm tree, rainbow, and peacock.
Setting: Slides of East Africa, South Africa and West Africa (Liberia) may be projected on the back wall of stage, or on a screen at rear. The three different houses—veld-style, Masai and Vai—may be cut-outs of painted cardboard. Masai houses are long, low and plastered, and are entered by crawling. Veld houses vary; some are beehive-shaped, and others have circular walls with thatched roofs. The Vai house is round with a tall, pointed, thatched roof. Houses may have working doorways.
Lighting: No special effects.

THE MONKEY WITHOUT A TAIL

Characters: 2 male; 1 female; 3 male or female for Attendant, Storyteller, Monkey, and 1 or 2 male or female for Mej; as many Subjects as desired.
Playing Time: 20 minutes.
Costumes: Draped robes in the style of Amhara people of Ethiopia (use sheets); King and Queen wear crowns. Attendant may carry a

fringed umbrella to hold over King's head. Monkey and Mej wear animal costumes (Monkey has no tail), or they may wear tights with matching turtleneck sweaters and papier-mâché heads. Mej wears a rope bridle and a rope sling to hold honey jar.

Properties: Large pottery jars; brilliantly painted jar for Monkey. (Jars may be made of papier-mâché or suggested by cardboard cut-outs.)

Setting: A dark backdrop curtain. In scene 1, forest, cut-outs of palm and acacia trees with ferns are scattered upstage. Left center are two stools covered to look like stones, and a fire, suggested by sticks of wood and crushed red and yellow cellophane. The two thrones in Scene 2, the Palace, may be made by taping cardboard boxes around arms and backs of chairs and painting them gold and other vivid colors in geometric designs.

Lighting: No special effects.

Sound: Drumbeats as indicated in text.

BATA'S LESSONS

Characters: 7 male; 5 female; and 1 male or female voice for Narrator. Palm and Acacia are non-speaking roles.

Playing Time: 20 minutes.

Costumes: Ancient Egyptian dress. For women, long tunics, and for men, wraparound skirts (made of old sheets), belted with bright material. Wide, painted, cardboard collars are worn by all but trees and soldiers. Lotus in Scene 2 and Pharaoh have collars made of gold and jewels. Gods wear headdresses, with black yarn attached for hair, and the following symbols: Ra, sun disk; Ament, hawk;

Isis, throne; Khnum, ram's head with wavy horns; and Bata in Scene 2, bull's head. Lotus wears a yellow wig, with a lotus-flower wreath in Scene 1 and at end of play, and a crown in Scene 2. Pharaoh wears traditional "double crown" (see costume book for illustration) and has a beard. Black yarn wigs are worn by Anpu, Soldiers, and Bata in Scene 1 and at end of play. Trees wear brown or black shirts and pants, with branches, made of paper or cloth and wire from clothes hangers, attached to arms, shoulders and head.

Properties: Three sheathed wooden swords, lotus-flower wreath, papyrus reed (made of paper), goblet.

Setting: Ancient Egypt. A painting of the river Nile extends across backdrop and stage, dividing playing area into two sections. There is a yellow backdrop, with river painted on it extending from ceiling height at right to stage level at left, gradually widening. River is painted across stage floor as if continuing downstage into audience. Against backdrop at right and center are small cardboard cut-outs of pyramids as if seen from a distance. For Scene 2, outside Pharaoh's palace, there are two folding screens at center, at an angle to represent corner of palace and placed so they encompass most of river area on stage floor. Left exit leads into palace and right exit leads into city.

Lighting: Blackouts, as indicated in text.

Sound: Egyptian music and bells tinkling for desert crossing. Narrator speaks into a glass for hollow effect and may be backstage or hidden at foot of stage. If voice not loud enough, use microphone.

TRICKSTER HARE'S FEAST

Characters: 1 male; 4 female; 8 male or female for animals and Three Merchants.
Playing Time: 20 minutes.
Costumes: African dress for Kagwa, Nambi, Merchants and Washer Women. Animals wear head masks with strips of raffia attached to bottom of masks and extending to floor.
Properties: Two bundles of cloth (one dirty); bundles of clothing; load of wood; five banana leaves.
Setting: Scene 1: Marketplace in Uganda. Umbrella tree may be painted on backdrop. On three colorful cloths spread out on stage are plantains, cooking pots and knives, and sweet potatoes. At center is a sawhorse frame with five prop chickens—four plump, one skinny—hanging on it. One chicken has leg that can be removed. Scene 2: Hare's compound. Large double gate with closing bar is up left. Right center is cardboard cutout of thatched house. Doorway is covered with hanging cloth. In front of house is a drum. Kettle, ax, and knife are upstage.
Lighting: No special effects.
Sound: Hare plays drum, as indicated in text.

THE GREAT TUG OF WAR

Characters: 8 male or female.
Playing Time: About 20 minutes.
Costumes: Animals wear papier mâché heads or makeup and attachments to face. Villagers wear togas and beaded jewelry.
Properties: African-style mat; pipe; small stool; long rope.
Setting: Painted backdrop of village and grasslands. Cardboard cut-

outs of acacia trees and bushes. Large circle of gray paper for water hole.
Lighting: Rosy glow indicating sunrise. Blackouts as indicated between Scenes 1 and 2 and at the end.

MANTIS, THE DREAMER

Characters: 1 male; 2 female; 4 male or female for Kwammanga, Mongoose, Cub, and Eland.
Playing Time: 15 minutes.
Costumes: Faces painted to indicate animal characters with covered wire attachments for ears, antennae, and antlers, plus loops of yarn for lion's mane. Kwammanga has a cardboard headdress, painted like a rainbow. All wear black tights and T-shirts.
Properties: Bag large enough for Mantis to get into and hide (cloth painted in imitation of a leather bag); chunks of meat (pieces of styrofoam painted to look like meat).
Setting: Painted backdrop of Kalahari Desert of South Africa. Cardboard cutouts of bushes around a water hole (blue paper circle) and a *scherm* (hut that Bushmen make from branches and grass) with doorway cut for use as entrance and exit.
Lighting: No special effects.
Sound: Mantis jumping into water hole and splashing about (drop rock in bucket of water and thrash about—best if amplified), as indicated in text.

TWO FROM ABUNUWAS

Characters: 3 male; 2 female; and 2 male or female for Storyteller and Donkey.
Playing Time: 20 minutes.
Costumes: North African. Men and

women wear robes and sandals. Women's robes are dark, with matching shawls draped over heads and pulled across faces and tossed over one shoulder. Only their eyes show; they either must speak loudly or move the veil slightly aside. Men have head scarves and headbands to hold them in place; they wear beards and mustaches, white for Abunuwas, black for Haji and Ali. Donkey wears a papier mâché head and grey costume with a yarn tail.

Properties: Small oriental rug, pair of sandals, two large cooking pots (one obviously old, the other new), one small old cooking pot.

Setting: Backdrop painting of Sahara Desert in Northern Africa with edge of village, flat-roofed, white houses. Two free-standing palm trees may be made from long curved sticks set in flag pole stands, topped with fronds made of fringed green paper attached to pieces of wire (straightened coat hangers), and, just beneath the base of the fronds, date clusters made from brown paper. For the rock, the sides of a low table may be covered with brown wrapping paper.

Lighting: Blackouts, as indicated in text.

WHO WEARS THE NECKLACE NOW?

Characters: 13 or more male and female.

Playing Time: 20 minutes.

Costumes: Storyteller and Warrior wear traditional Masai red cloth wraparounds thrown over one shoulder, sandals and jewelry (including imitation ear plugs of cardboard). Warrior has shoulder pouch, and carries spear. Hare, Antelope, Elephant, and Hyenas have their faces painted to look like the animals, and papier mâché or cloth-covered wire ears attached to their heads. Elephant has an ears-and-trunk contraption tied on head. Fire is dressed in red and yellow with flame-shaped paper attached to cap. Waterhole wears khaki safari outfit and lies under blue blanket. Termite Hill wears full-length brown cone-shaped costume with a hole in front for face. Acacia Tree wears brown and carries real or imitation acacia branches. Chorus may wear modern dress or Masai costumes.

Properties: Gourd rattle, spearhead.

Setting: Backdrop painting of Southern Kenya bush country. Vine-like rope appears to grow along ground up right.

Sound: Rattle is shaken by Storyteller to accompany chants, when indicated in script.